SECRETS
OF THE
MASTER
SALES
MANAGERS

SECRETS
OF THE
MASTER
SALES
MANAGERS

PORTER HENRY

American Management Association

New York • Atlanta • Boston • Chicago • Kansas City • San Francisco • Washington, D.C.
Brussels • Toronto • Mexico City

This publication is designed to provide accurate and authoritative
information in regard to the subject matter covered. It is sold with
the understanding that the publisher is not engaged in rendering
legal, accounting, or other professional service. If legal advice or
other expert assistance is required, the services of a competent
professional person should be sought.

Library of Congress Cataloging-in-Publication Data

Henry, Porter.
    Secrets of the master sales managers / [interviewer Porter Henry].
       p.   cm.
    Includes index.
    ISBN 0-8144-0221-6
    1. Sales management.   I. Title.
    HF5438.4.H46   1993
    658.8'1—dc20   93-13755
                                                                         CIP

Printing number

10   9   8   7   6   5   4   3   2   1

Contents

Preface

This book is written by sales managers, for sales managers.

Specifically it is addressed to the first-line sales manager—the person to whom the salespeople directly report. In larger companies, this is usually the district sales manager. In smaller companies, this is often the sales manager. In still smaller companies, with only two or three salespeople, this is often the president or owner.

Whatever the size of the company, the role of the first-line sales manager is the key to the success of the selling side of marketing activity.

Some years ago the Life Insurance Institute made a study of the first-line manager's influence upon the success of the sales representative. They classified a large number of trainees into candidates who rated A on their initial aptitude tests and those who rated B or lower. They also classified the first-line managers to whom these fledgling salespeople reported into the "best half" and the "lower" half of managers. Note that these were all experienced and successful managers—but it's always possible to sort any group into the upper half and the lower half.

Then they tracked the success of these new sales reps over a period of several years. The percentage of new sellers who became successful career life insurance sales reps was this:

	Percentage Successful Under "Best Half" Managers	*Percentage Successful Under "Lower Half" Managers*
A candidates	65%	35%
B or lower	35	13

The astonishing result of this study was that a "poor" salesperson under a good manager was as likely to succeed as a "top" salesperson under a not-so-good manager. In short, the quality of the manager is as important a factor in a sales rep's success as intelligence, motivation, communication skills, and all the other factors mentioned in the predictive tests.

Ask any really outstanding sales rep about the secret of his or her success, and very often the answer will start with "You see, I had this great sales manager back when I was starting out. . . ."

How This Book Was Written

So it seemed desirable to let first-line sales managers—many of them since promoted to higher sales executive positions—exchange practical suggestions on handling the many functions they perform.

This book is a true symposium. Twenty-seven sales managers, in a wide variety of companies, were selected as contributors. A brief summary of each chapter was mailed to them, and they responded with additional ideas, suggestions, comments, even disagreements. (Two contributors learned, after participating, that their companies did not want them to be identified. Hence they are titled Communications Sales Manager and Computer Sales Manager in this book.)

The author is indebted to these sales managers for their thoughtful contributions to this book. Their detailed biographies are found at the end of the book. Here are their names and affiliations:

Selling to Business Industry

Aspen Technology, Craig Hattabaugh
Cellular One, David M. Singer
Communications Sales Manager
Computer Sales Manager
Datacard Corp., Tom Dunning
Dow Chemical USA, Jim Nichols
FlexCon & Systems, Inc., Daniel R. Schnaars
GTE, Robert G. McCoy
Monsanto Agricultural Company, Frank P. Schneemann and Kevin A. Flagel
NCR, Patrick G. Murphy, D. M. House, and Robert S. Layman
Olsten Temporaries, Lori Schweitzer-Teismann
United States Cellular, Jack L. Woods

Selling for Resale (to Wholesalers or Dealers)

American Greetings, Tim Duncan
The Clorox Company, Alina Bilodeau
Heinz U.S.A., G. A. (Jerry) McCloskey
McKesson Drug Co., Bill Hammick
Nabisco Foods Group, Charles Williamson

Selling to the Consumer

Allstate Insurance, Alex Jones
Amway, Stan Evans and Ruth Evans
Mary Kay Cosmetics, Judie McCoy
Merrill Lynch, David A. Ruckman
Terminix International, Howard Strelsin
United Homecraft, William G. Nyberg

Selling to Doctors and Hospitals

CIBA, Robert Higham
G. D. Searle, V. N. (Andy) Anderson

1

Sales Management as a Career

The role of the first-line sales manager is unique in the corporate hierarchy. Time pressures on this manager are terrific: from above, demands for special investigations and reports as well as the routine paperwork; from the side, customers, trade or professional organizations, and community activities; and from below, sales reps who never get enough attention.

Yet in most companies, this busy manager is usually the only executive who doesn't have a private secretary (unless the job also involves managing a warehouse or a service operation).

As indicated by some of the remarks below, many first-line managers tend to feel somewhat overworked and unappreciated, but they find that their biggest reward lies in the achievements of some of the salespeople they develop.

The feelings of many first-line managers are summed up by Tim Duncan of American Greetings: "Sales management as a career is not for everyone. It takes a rare breed to be successful in sales management over a long span of time. It is a job where 'burnout' is commonplace. Compare it with a front-line sergeant in the army: constantly receiving orders and being responsible for accomplishing the task with a group of people only as strong as the weakest individual.

"The sales manager really wears two hats. It is without doubt one of the most difficult and thankless careers one may choose, but also one of the most rewarding.

"A good guess is that only 10 percent of all sales managers retire from the position. They either burn out or are unable to keep up with the demands of the position.

"As always, though, the cream rises to the top. I currently have two managers who have been in their positions for twenty-plus years. They are classified as strong trainers and have something in common: they enjoy developing people. They gave up on personal recognition for recognition of their unit, the sales district. They get more enjoyment from the success of their people than from their own. After all, when their people are successful so are they.

"One of these managers compares it with gardening—'You only reap what you sow. A new sales representative is like a young plant. You carefully set the roots, fertilize, water, and protect it from harm, and before long they can make it on their own. Then they begin to thrive. They are successful with a minimum of your effort and you're proud of them for what they've become.

"The other manager approaches it as parenting. 'Treat them all as your own and each the same. Care for them and treat them with respect, and they will respect you. Love them, kick them if you must, then love them again.'

"As for me, I think it is the greatest career out there. I couldn't think of anything I would enjoy more."

Echoing the last sentiment, Tom Dunning of Datacard Corp. says, "Sales management has been good to me. 'Dayton, Ohio, boy makes good!' I don't know how sales management as a profession compares with law or medicine because I've not been there nor do I care to be. Having my living depend upon criminals and sick people does not appeal to me. If my children are mentally suited to sales as a career, I would recommend it. Being a success at anything requires an honest evaluation of one's capabilities and then capitalizing on one's assets."

"The manager needs to understand that the primary goal is to develop people, not to simply go out and make a daily quota of sales," notes David Singer of Cellular One. "You can make or break the entire career of a person by how well you work with him or her in your role as a first-line manager.

"The transition from sales rep to first-line manager is tough. You need to use the skill you developed out there in the field plus a whole new set of management skills. You need an internal drive to be successful, because it's an underappreciated role."

"The chief role of the sales manager," adds the Communications Sales Manager, "is to focus the abilities and energies of the sales rep toward the target of profits. Managers get a big reward in seeing the success of the reps they have developed. Sometimes it's tough for the manager to see a rep move further up the line than the manager did.

Another aspect of sales management as a career is that it offers an opportunity for exposure to other corporate functions if the manager is considering a career change. The sales manager can evaluate a career in general management, R&D, HQ staff, manufacturing, service, and others.

"The working personality of a front-line manager is very important," notes Charles Williamson of Nabisco Foods Group. "The manager must radiate enthusiasm, must have and instill a positive mental attitude. He or she must be available at all times for the needs of the sales force. The manager must gain their respect by never asking more than the manager would be willing to do. The manager must be forceful enough to require the sales reps to do their very best at all times.

"The manager must offer constructive criticism in private but praise in writing. The manager must insist that each member of the group continue to grow and learn through books, tapes, and seminars. The manager must assist in setting goals and then assist in reaching those goals. The manager must act instead of reacting, to teach and reward leadership."

G. A. McCloskey of Heinz U.S.A. feels that "a career in sales that leads to sales management is an exciting way to develop one's personal worth. A good sales manager touches upon many facets of the business world. Be it forecasting, finance, production, shipping, or customer interaction, the sales manager becomes a business unit—a mini-corporate unit that gels all portions of our business to fulfill our business obligations.

"The rewards are many, including some internal satisfactions that can be understood only by 'being there.' Drawbacks are hard to anticipate as the job fluctuates daily. Time, composition, and changes in the company's goals and personalities make adaptability and flexibility an important part of the sales manager's character."

"The first-line manager is the counterbalance between the needs of the individual and the needs of the organization," adds Jack Woods of United States Cellular. "You need to be one brick short to take on the job, but it's the most rewarding career available because of the mixture of activities on a day-to-day basis. You get less money and more headaches than some of the members of your sales team, but the intangible rewards are more important than the compensation."

How Can a Sales Manager Improve?

Given the importance of this position, how can the first-line manager improve his or her ability to cope with it? Surprisingly, hundreds of books are written about the skills of the sales reps who report to this manager, and hundreds more are written about the skills of the top executives to whom the first-line manager reports, but there is barely a handful of books about the skills required of the first-line manager.

Managers can gain something from books and seminars about management skills in general (if they can translate the basics to the specifics of their own position), but essentially they learn from one another.

"One of the most important ways managers can learn to be better managers is to hold rap sessions among themselves," says Andy Anderson of G. D. Searle. "At each quarterly meeting that the regional directors hold for managers, we urge them to set aside half a day without the regional director being there, just to swap ideas and problems. We got that idea from Marvin Rafal."

"Always observe, learn and adapt," recommends the Communications Sales Manager. "Whether in the role of a peer, a supervisor, or a subordinate, the manager can learn things, both positively and negatively. No one seminar, individual, or book has the one answer. It takes constant observation."

A method of simultaneously developing both managers and sellers is described by Howard Strelsin of Terminix International: "I have a theory of what I call the training gap. There are several skills that are important for a salesperson to master: time management skills, organizational skills, presentation skills, product knowledge skills, closing skills, and creative prospecting skills.

"I go into a branch and ask the manager to evaluate himself and each of his reps on those skills and also get the sales reps to evaluate themselves *and the manager* on those skills.

"Now you compare them. If the manager feels his great strength is in, say, product knowledge and there are reps who rate themselves low in product knowledge, that identifies a training gap. The manager has all this knowledge and has not imparted it to the reps. As division sales manager, my job is to make sure that over the next several weeks the manager transfers this product knowledge to the sales force.

"Another kind of gap is revealed when the manager identifies one skill as his area of weakness and the sales reps feel that it's their greatest weakness as well. The manager can't teach reps to manage their time if he can't manage his own. The manager needs to improve his own weak area in order to be more valuable to his people. He improves this area by studying about or seeking help from the divisional or regional manager."

One Manager's Experience

One manager's experience in developing his own managerial development program is described by Tim Duncan of American Greetings: "In my first sales management position [with a previous company], I was unfortunate in that I had no formal training and a supervisor who worked with me only twice a year. I was forced into self-development or no development.

"The first thing I had going for me was day-to-day experience, and I learned a lot from that. I tried not to make mistakes, but when I did I made sure I learned something from the experience.

"My first action was to call on my peers and past supervisors. I learned a lot by talking things through with them and even creating hypothetical situations to discuss. It was comforting to find that my decisions matched theirs; this gave me confidence to make future decisions.

"I also learned a great deal from talking with my customers, since they were managers too. This also helped me develop rapport with them. I was careful to make sure that the subjects I discussed with them were appropriate.

"I also went to the library and asked the librarian and others using the business library about good books and tapes I could use. There were several reference books available that listed thousands of books, articles, and tapes. I started reading books such as *The One-Minute Manager* and listening to self-help tapes while driving.

"I got the idea of asking my sales reps what more I could do to help them. I used their feedback to determine what I did that helped them and what seemed useless to them. I used this on each rep, as I found that I got different answers from different sales reps. This confirmed my belief that all my sales reps were different, learned differently, and were motivated differently from one another.

"One thing that most managers seem to forget is to sharpen their own sales abilities. One thing I always try to do is to teach each sales rep something new each time I work with that rep. By sharpening my own skills, I can teach them new things.

"My boss recently gave me a self-improvement course called 'Commitment to Excellence' by the Professional Information Group of Simon and Schuster. It is a self-evaluation and goal-setting process that has helped me a great deal. Another great self-help tool is a *Harvard Business Review* issue titled 'People: Managing Your Most Important Asset.'

"One last idea is to use professional organizations such as Toastmasters or Dale Carnegie courses. I attended a few lectures by Charles Givens and I did attend a free introductory course of an organization similar to Dale Carnegie, but it didn't help me. Those kinds of classes are great short-term motivators for me, but after a few days or weeks the fire usually goes out. I compare them to those get-rich-quick people you see on television interviewing people from Hawaii who successfully completed their course and got rich quick too."

2

Recruiting New Sales Representatives

"Probably the most important and most difficult task in effectively hiring top-quality salespeople is the everyday recruiting that is necessary," comments Alex Jones of Allstate Insurance Company.

"Most sales organizations, regardless of size, cannot accurately predict turnover, which causes the need for replacement. To eliminate hurry-up hiring, it is imperative that a sales manager have a log of qualified candidates to choose from when the need arises.

"As Vince Lombardi said about winning, 'Recruiting is not a some-time thing, it is an all-time thing' if a sales manager is to be effective in building an organization."

Dave Singer of Cellular One agrees. "Recruiting is one of the single most important aspects of being a first-line manager," he says, "because the sustainment of your business depends upon your ability to attract good people."

"The manager lives and dies by finding new reps," notes Tom Dunning of Datacard Corp. "You must recruit all the time, but you can't force it. If the person doesn't 'go' on the first interview, don't force it. Managers and reps work so closely together that there has to be a good chemical reaction between them. So don't force it."

"Surround yourself with the best people possible. Pay the premium price when necessary, then manage by allowing them to get the job done their way." That's the advice Tim Duncan of American Greetings received from his superior when he was a new manager, and to this day he believes "that really says it all."

"I remember the pressure I felt to get a quality person when hiring my first sales rep," he recalls. "I received this great advice from my supervisor: people management isn't so difficult if you believe and follow the right philosophy. Of course you need to guide and advise your reps on occasion, but you hired them to do the job, so now let them get to work. You may not always be able to afford the premium; in that case, find the person hungry for experience with the most on the ball."

The Importance of Recruiting

The success of any sales force is largely dependent upon the quality of the salesmen and saleswomen it recruits. No training program, no motivational carrots can make a top producer out of a dud.

This does not imply that there is some magic "sales personality" or a pool of "natural-born sellers." But by analyzing its own outstanding producers, a company can determine what kinds of drives, interests, values, and experiences they have in common.

Most companies need a continuous infusion of new trainees, not only to expand the sales force but also to replace existing salespeople lost through promotions, retirements, resignations, or the pirating of competitors.

The more candidates the company runs through its selection process, the better. If you wanted a very tall salesperson, you'd certainly do better with the tallest of twenty-five applicants than with the taller of two.

In most companies the first-line manager is responsible for finding the recruits necessary to fill vacancies in the district. Even in very large companies, which do most of their recruiting at the headquarters level, it does no harm to the manager's career to become known as a good recruiter of topnotch sales candidates.

Before Recruiting: Job Descriptions and Person Profiles

An indispensable guide to anyone involved in recruiting is an accurate job description or position description. "It's a must," says Craig Hattabaugh of Aspen Technology. "It serves as a foundation for recruitment tools such as advertisements, and if corporate people are involved it helps co-ordinate internal resources."

If the company doesn't provide a job or position description, it's worth the local manager's time to write one. If the company does have one, the manager should review it to make sure it is up-to-date, covers all the facets of the job, and doesn't require any tailoring to fit the specifics of the territory.

The job description (see Figures 2-1 and 2-2) basically covers:

1. The person to whom the sales rep reports.
2. The type of selling involved: what kinds of products or services are sold, to what types of prospects or customers.
3. Sales support work involved, such as merchandising, setting up displays, writing proposals, performing installation, or service work.
4. Reports prepared and received.
5. Equipment provided, such as company autos and demonstrators.
6. Method of compensation.
7. Potential career paths.

"A sales position, with many companies, involves more than just selling," notes Charles Williamson of Nabisco Foods Group. "To recruit and keep a successful salesperson, any additional responsibilities must be addressed at the beginning.

"The job description should include a schedule of the selling hours and the evening hours required for sales preparation and administrative work. It also should mention any additional work that will be needed from time to time to maintain the sales territory—for example, the physical labor in store resets. It should also outline the amount of daily and overnight travel required.

"A thorough job description gives an overview of what is expected from the position. This will eliminate any 'surprises' that can demotivate a new employee."

Robert McCoy of GTE points out that the job description should define the type of selling to be done: whether it is *transactional* selling, which tends to be short term, small value, with the focus on price, or *strategic* selling, which is long term, relationship-based, with the focus on added value.

Adds the Communications Sales Manager: "The job description also needs to clearly identify the types of quantifiable objectives the new sales rep will be expected to attain—net results, not just efforts."

"If the job description describes the functions in detail, you may want to add an ambiguous phrase such as 'and other assigned duties,' " cautions Tim Duncan of American Greetings. "Some individuals, especially those with blue-collar backgrounds, may try to hold you to each word of the job description.

Figure 2-1. Sample job description for sales representative.

TERMINIX INTERNATIONAL, INC.
JOB DESCRIPTION

JOB TITLE __Sales Representative__ JOB NUMBER __4570__

SALARY GRADE _____

DIVISION _____ LOCATION (BRANCH) _____ DEPARTMENT __Sales__

REPORTS TO (TITLE) __Branch Sales Supervisor or Branch Manager__

SUMMARY OF RESPONSIBILITIES:

Conduct inspections to identify infestations, or conditions conducive to infestations, of wood-destroying organisms and/or insects, birds, or other vertebrate pests, for the purpose of making proposals and presentations to obtain sales contracts for the Company's respective services to owners or agents of property inspected.

SPECIFIC DUTIES:

1. Sell termite control protection and renewals, and/or monthly pest control protection, to homes, stores, and industry.
2. Cover sales leads in assigned territory.
3. By creative effort, develop at least three termite, or four pest control, sales leads for each respective office lead furnished.
4. Record accurate measurements, and write correct descriptions of property inspected.
5. Prepare appropriate specifications and treating instructions in accordance with existing laws, regulations, and Company Policy.
6. Compute job treating cost from company pricing instructions.
7. Execute contracts on behalf of the Company, observing Company Policy as to credit terms of sales.
8. Supervise collection effort on delinquent accounts of personal sales contracts.
9. Advise customers about other Terminix services.
10. Deal courteously with customers.
11. Leave customers's premises and furnishings clean and as found.
12. Contact customers after service is performed to ensure customer satisfaction and to develop additional prospects.
13. Report any unusual requests from customers or questions you cannot answer to your immediate supervisor.
14. Maintain prospect and call-back files.
15. Maintain sales activity records.
16. Maintain equipment and vehicle in a state of cleanliness and good working order.
17. Maintain and use personal safety equipment issued.
18. Examine architectural drawings and specifications, and prepare estimates for soil pre-treatment bids.
19. Complete appropriate training courses.
20. Know the location and phone number of local poison control centers.
21. Participate in public relations and promotional efforts as required.
22. Perform other duties as assigned.

SUPERVISION GIVEN: _____

SUPERVISION RECEIVED: General supervision; plans and arranges own work in the performance of a sequence of operations, referring unusual matters to supervisor as necessary.

Figure 2-2.   Sample job description for sales manager.

POSITION DESCRIPTION: Division Sales Manager

REPORTS TO: Divisional Vice President (Indirect)
                                           National Sales Director (Direct)

SUMMARY OF RESPONSIBILITIES:

Works with and through Regional Managers to accomplish all company sales objectives.

SPECIFIC DUTIES:

1. Assist in the planning and budgeting of Divisional sales goals.
2. Increase unit sales, sales volume, and market share through the implementation, teaching, and enforcement of company sales policies.
3. Monitor and assure adequate sales staffing in all branches.
4. Monitor and assure compliance of company sales training programs.
5. Develop and implement motivational programs, sales promotions, sales contests, and seminars to enhance company loyalty and increase sales production.
6. Monitor and assure adequate pricing practices and existing rate card compliance in all branches.
7. Maintain regular contact with Regional Managers on sales programs relative to staffing, training, pricing, production, etc.
8. Assist in developing, modifying, and implementing sales policies and procedures.
9. Develop and implement programs that will increase sales and generate leads from all service technicians in the division.
10. Evaluate marketing potential in all branches. Make recommendations on branch splits and improved market penetration to the Divisional Vice President and National Sales Director.
11. Serve as liaison between the marketing department and National Sales Department, and all field operations to ensure proper interpretation of marketing policies, yellow pages, P.O.S. literature, etc.
12. Serve as liaison between the National Accounts Department and all field operations to ensure proper communications and interpretation of marketing policies.
13. Monitor and assure the safeguarding of all company equipment, property, and facilities.
14. Monitor and assure a top-quality image with all equipment, property, facilities, and personnel.
15. Set an excellent example and quality image to all company personnel and the public.

"A newly hired sales rep once told me he wasn't required to work any Saturday mornings because that wasn't in his job description. He also said that attending the grand openings of new stores wasn't there either. I was forced to use other motivational tactics in this situation, but it could have been easily avoided if the job description had been worded differently."

Based on the description of the job, it is desirable to prepare a Person Profile that answers the question: What type of person does it take to do this work? In many cases this profile is based on an analysis of the company's outstanding sellers.

As noted by J. J. Nichols of Dow Chemical USA: "Recruiting and training sales representatives can be a very expensive process. Therefore it is important to do it right the first time. One approach is to examine the demographics and personality traits of successful sellers employed by your company. In that information you may find a guide for recruiting new sellers."

The profile also lists the <u>necessary</u> age, education, experience, and other prerequisites, such as the ability to drive a truck, speak a second language, or whatever. The word *necessary* is underlined because this document describes the minimum qualifications, not the one-in-a-lifetime ideal background.

"Although the profile is important, be flexible and deviate from it when your instincts tell you to," suggests Craig Hattabaugh of Aspen Technology. "Some of our top salespeople didn't fit the profile."

"We try to find people who have niches," reports David Ruckman of Merrill Lynch. "We look for sales reps who have a natural affinity with groups. For instance, we hired a Korean fellow a while back, we've hired a rabbi, we've hired a lawyer, we've hired a CPA, we've hired a Lebanese fellow, with a direct view toward pointing these people toward a natural affinity where they have contacts and connections and common grounds and in some cases speak the language. We hired a young fellow who speaks Russian fluently, because in Cleveland there are many Russian immigrants in the Jewish community."

To avoid being sued for alleged discrimination by an unsuccessful applicant, be sure that the profile contains only job-related qualifications. Don't specify "male" unless you're sure that a woman couldn't handle the job. And remember that it's illegal to discriminate, for reasons of age, against anyone from 40 to 70 years of age.

Sources of Recruits

A recruitment method that works well in big cities may be less effective in rural areas; last year's hot source of recruits may be a dry well this year.

So most sales managers use several methods of recruiting and keep up-to-date records on the number of applicants, and the number of successful candidates, from each source.

"In considering sources of recruits," suggests Jack Woods of United States Cellular, "keep in mind the environment in which the new reps will work. I have some reps calling on professional people and others calling on construction workers. I wouldn't use the same source to fill such different types of positions."

The Constant "Bird Dog"

Foresighted managers are always on the lookout for possible candidates, even when there is not an immediate opening in the sales force. They may spot a likely looking recruit at a church or club activity, in the seat next to them on a plane, among the vendors who call on them, even among customers or clients.

They may not mention the possibility to the "suspect," or they may explain that "we don't have an opening on our sales force right now, but when we do, would you be interested in considering a position with us?"

In either event, the name is squirreled away with a growing list of possible applicants to be contacted when recruits are needed.

"Recruiting is not something you do when you need somebody," says Alex Jones of Allstate. "It's something you do continually, year in and year out.

"For example, when I get a phone call from somebody selling securities or real estate or whatever, I listen patiently, see what their skills are, and determine if I'd like to invite them in for an interview. I've found some good people that way.

"The same thing applies to walk-in salespeople selling copying machines or stationery. This is a form of selection as well as recruiting because you get to see them in action and size them up."

"If you are continually recruiting," adds Dave Singer of Cellular One, "you have the luxury of picking from a larger pool of candidates."

Bill Hammick of McKesson Drug takes note of the manufacturer's reps who call on him, because "they can identify with our business." He also mentions an unusual source: in a department store or home entertainment center, he gives the floor salespeople a chance to try to sell him something. If they make an enthusiastic presentation, he asks if they'd be interested in furthering their sales career.

A good example of the constant recruiter is Judie McCoy of Mary Kay Cosmetics. Her firm invites women to attend demonstrations of their facial products in a customer's home.

"When they see what we're doing they're enthusiastic, it appeals to them, but most of the time they're not even thinking about selling— so we ask them. We look for recruits in our classes for facials, but we're like head hunters; we're always looking for people with certain qualities.

"I was out for dinner one night and ran into someone I had not seen since grade school. She was in a management position with a utility company but wasn't getting anywhere. I looked at her and saw enthusiasm, wonderful people skills, it is obvious she really liked people, and she was ambitious, not afraid to work. We talked it over and she became a brand new director for Mary Kay.

"There's a big difference between a person who's a good salesperson and one who is also a good recruiter. In Mary Kay you have to be both to be successful. The people who are good at sales but not at recruiting are the ones who don't see beyond the faces. The recruiters are the ones who get into the inside of the person.

"Today most women are working, so their first objection is that they don't have time for selling. I work out a weekly plan for them to show them where they can find enough time to build a business.

"If a woman has a full-time job, there's a risk involved in giving it up, so she usually starts on a part-time basis. But not always. I recruited a woman who taught at a local university. She was fed up with her job, fed up with her income, so she quit her job and came into Mary Kay full-time from day one. Today she has won a Mary Kay pink Cadillac as an outstanding producer.

"I could care less where a person is coming from, I only care about where she wants to go. Lots of people want to be successful, but very few are willing to work for it. My basic philosophy is that you can take a willing person and make her capable, but you can't take a capable person and make her willing."

Clients or Customers

Lori Schweitzer-Teismann of Olsten Temporaries in Cincinnati points out that it is sometimes practical to recruit new sales reps from clients.

"Users, at least in the temporary help industry, make excellent sales reps," she says. "It would cause problems to directly approach a person you perceive to be an excellent candidate and in essence 'steal' one of your client's top employees. Also, if a client's employee applies for a sales position and is rejected, you could lose a top client as a result of hard feelings.

"One way to approach a current client is to plant a seed by saying, 'Our company has an opening for a salesperson doing essentially what I do. Do you know of anyone who might be interested?' Four of our five current vice-presidents were formerly our day-to-day contacts within client firms."

An example of hiring from a customer is contributed by Tim Duncan of American Greetings. "As a sales representative, I sold an independent retailer on using American Greetings as the main supplier. As we were setting up the card shop, a young lady came in and asked for a job as clerk. The owner hired her. As we were working to open up the store, I noticed her unusual drive in completing tasks. After the store opened, she sold nearly every customer who entered the store. Her suggestive selling and add-on sales were great.

"Three months later I was promoted to sales management and when my first territory in that area opened, I hired her. She turned out to be a great asset and did an excellent job managing a territory for me."

Intern Programs

Some companies have found it desirable to recruit candidates for temporary "intern" positions rather than place them directly into the sales force.

For example, Howard Strelsin of Terminix International says: "We are constantly advertising for 'management trainees.' For many of these people, selling is the first step up the management ladder, and some of them become excellent salespeople. They may find that they prefer selling to managing, although they might not have responded to an ad for salespeople."

The Computer Sales Manager reports that his company has developed a Sales Intern Program that is highly successful. Because his company is selling a very technical computer application service, it was not easy, prior to the development of the intern program, to hire experienced sales reps from outside the company.

"We would hire salespeople with three to five years' experience, give them a training program, and put them out into the field selling a very technical product. Often we made a good hire, but there were other times when the new reps were so set in their ways that they never really grasped the way we wanted to do business. The time required to learn our product and understand all the facets of the business was much longer than we or the new reps wanted. Many of them had left highly productive jobs and expected to equal or improve their earnings in a short time, and that was not always possible.

"Another difficulty with traditional hiring methods was that no matter how thoroughly we interviewed a recruit, we were never sure how well he or she would perform on the job. We did not get a chance to see them in action.

"Someone at [company] was smart enough five years ago to develop our present Sales Intern Program. We go to major business schools and recruit the top students who are planning a career in selling. For example, in my Atlanta area we recruit at Georgia, Georgia Tech, and Georgia State universities, interviewing thirty to forty individuals a year and selecting from one to four.

"We put them into a two-year training program during which they are holding down real jobs, but jobs without a sales quota to meet. For example, an intern might become:

- An account executive, who gains an in-depth knowledge of our products by installing them and training our clients in their use
- A marketing rep, whose duties involve telemarketing, phone surveys, market research, making appointments for sales reps, and otherwise assisting the sales and marketing teams

"During this transition period they learn [company] philosophies, our work requirements, and the technical aspects of our products. They also learn a lot about selling by attending all the sales training sessions and sales meetings that the sales force attends.

"The entire program is highly structured to ensure that they learn at the proper rate, that they do have a meaningful job, that they are monitored and developed by the management team.

"Meanwhile we get a firsthand knowledge of their motivation and work habits and know just how fast we can bring them along. Some join the regular sales force after a six-month internment, some not for two years.

"Although there is some risk in investing this much training effort in college graduates, we have experienced a very low turnover among them.

"I normally have six to eight interns in some phase of the program, so I have excellent bench strength. If I lose a salesperson, I can select an intern and have the territory covered in a matter of days.

"Results of the program, in terms of sales productivity, have been phenomenal. Our sales force in the Atlanta area is now made up predominantly of these intern graduates. Some of our top sellers are only 26 or 27 years old. They are young, aggressive, eager to learn, and very manageable and coachable.

"I would always use an intern-type program to develop a sales force, regardless of where it would be. The program we use now is far superior to our old conventional methods of bringing in salespeople."

Recruiting Services

Recruiting firms like The Lenman Group and National Career Centers recruit 500 to 1,000 candidates to attend an interview session with 12 to 16 companies represented.

In some cases, companies seeking employees receive resumes from all candidates in advance of the meeting and designate those they wish to interview. Or a representative of each company may address the entire gathering before candidates choose the company they wish to contact.

Colleges

"What we do most often in our company is to recruit young college graduates right off the campus," reports J. J. Nichols of Dow Chemical USA.

"We train them in the culture of our company and in the methods we use to sell our products. This process takes about nine months before the recruit is given a field sales assignment."

Andy Anderson of G. D. Searle is not enthusiastic about college recruiting. "We're very active around the college campuses," he says, "but we don't hire many 'first-job' people that way. Only about 20 percent of our new reps are right out of college. College recruiting is hiring high turnover, in my experience."

A successful program for college recruiting is described by Pat Murphy of NCR Corporation. "By recruiting college seniors, on campus and prior to graduation, the professional sales recruiter has the best opportunity to employ the *best* and most competitive candidates ever.

"Case in point: University of Texas, Austin. More than one hundred college seniors attend a recruiter-sponsored on-campus function held from 6:30 to 9:00 P.M. the night before a day of scheduled 30-minute interviews.

"The recruiters are local NCR sales managers from Houston, Dallas, San Antonio, etc., who have reviewed the resumes of all graduates who have applied for the interviews. Only forty are scheduled for interviewing.

"Those local sales managers are trained in targeted selection. They will use the informal evening gathering to observe the behavior and mannerisms of the men and women present. They are looking to link up names and faces with respect to:

- Leaders in groups
- Leaders in mixed groups
- Loners with serious faces and questions
- Loners with "me too" faces
- Aggressive actors
- Leading actors

"These trained recruiters who manage the local offices are looking for employees who in five years will be the college alumni most recognized by their classmates. These best future alumni want to continue the status and values they have formed in school. They want jobs that:

- Make a lot of money
- Provide expense accounts
- Allow travel, possibly international
- Generate financial resources they can donate to the college scholarship funds, athletic clubs, fraternities, and sororities
- Put them in the best position for weekend campus reunions, football games, or homecoming activities

"The recruiter is planning to offer sales interviews to the *best* graduating people. If the recruiters get the best, any competitor and other recruiters will get weaker candidates, weaker leaders, and me-too faces.

"Long-term thinking about professional recruiting is a strategy that works. The power curve is sharp and probably out in front of most corporate personnel strategies."

Referrals From Sales Force

Many companies find that their own salespeople are good at finding sales recruits and even offer financial rewards for doing so. For example, Howard Strelsin explains that Terminix International gives a fifty-dollar bonus to any employee who refers a sales candidate who is employed and stays with the company for ninety days, another fifty dollars if the rep stays for six months, and a third fifty dollars if the rep is with the company for a year.

"In some instances," Strelsin notes, "the referring employee is responsible for some of the training the new person receives, and thus has a vested interest in his or her success."

"The key to finding new sales reps is networking through the current staff," agrees Andy Anderson of G. D. Searle. "We have what we call an 'employee-through-an-employee' program, where if a representative finds somebody we hire, we give the rep a bonus of up to $2,000. That's where we get most of our good people."

"I've been fortunate in recruiting people through the people who work here already," reports Bill Nyberg of United Homecraft. "Referrals are mostly from other salespeople, sometimes from someone working inside. We used to give $300 to a sales rep who referred a new sales rep that lasted six months, but discontinued it because we found it wasn't necessary."

Alex Jones of Allstate agrees. "I've found through nineteen years' experience that the best source of sales recruits is referrals from existing salespeople. The average salesperson does not want the manager to hire an individual who would project an unfavorable image on the company or the other personnel. This eliminates much of the danger of recruiting the wrong salesperson. It also makes your job of training the new person easier because the referring person will want to make sure that the individual he or she recommends becomes successful. They will be willing to provide some support to the new sales rep when the manager is unavailable."

"A major source of recruits is our present salespeople," says David A. Ruckman of Merrill Lynch. "We ask them whom they know who would do well in this business. We don't offer any monetary rewards; the motivation is the pride in saying, 'I brought that person into the industry and look how well he's doing.'

"The rep who brings in the new person usually takes a special interest in adding to his or her education and training, to make sure they succeed. It's a double whammy. If I hire someone from off the street I alone am responsible for making that person successful; if I hire a friend of an existing broker, I have someone who feels obligated to help me make that person successful.

"The person who did the referring can often help the new rep in a slump. The referrer knows more about the person's background and talents than I do, perhaps has a different approach in talking to him or her. We also find, by the way, that there are certain brokers who, if they advise you to hire somebody, have a 100 percent batting average."

From Within

Another source of recruits for many companies is the personnel of other company departments, such as production or customer service.

"I've found that the most stable and consistent salespeople we have in the company are those who came from our own service organization," reports Howard Strelsen of Terminix International. "These people have actually been delivering the service, so their sincerity, their belief in the product, comes across in their selling.

"We have some branches that even establish quotas for the number of service-to-sales transfers. When a salesperson leaves, the branch manager usually tries to replace him or her with a service person."

Among sources of recruits within the company itself, the Communications Sales Manager reminds us not to overlook:

+ Employees on an extended leave of absence
+ Entry-level customer service representatives

- Summer interns from local colleges
- Experienced salespersons who might possibly be transferred from other divisions of the company

"But," he cautions, "be sensitive to internal candidates requesting transfers. Their current boss may 'sell' you a prospect to rid themselves of a problem."

"Another source of recruits may be a division or a subsidiary that was sold off to another company," adds J. J. Nichols of Dow Chemical USA. "Recently we had an opening for an experienced seller. We placed an ad, and it was answered by a former employee of a division that had been sold to another company. He had gone with that division, then left it for what appeared to be a better job offer but found it didn't turn out as expected. With our knowledge of his successful sales background and his familiarity with our company, he was the perfect choice for our job opening."

Newspaper Ads

Newspaper ads are a common method of seeking sales recruits, but managers' evaluations of their effectiveness vary widely.

Bill Nyberg of United Homecraft says, "Newspaper ads are sometimes terrific, sometimes not. An ad will pull fine one week, and two weeks later it won't. You have to be consistent: run it and see what happens. Sometimes I'll run an ad when I don't need salespeople just to see what's out there. If it does unearth a good sales rep, I have to find a place for him or her."

Craig Hattabaugh of Aspen Technology has a more negative view. "Newspaper ads have not proven effective in recruiting for highly technical positions. Also, their results depend upon the health of the local economy. In New England during the 1980s, a $4,000 ad would yield one or two resumes. In the early 1990s, it yielded hundreds."

David A. Ruckman of Merrill Lynch says, "We do not do any newspaper advertising, never have found it effective."

Alex Jones of Allstate is perhaps the most negative. "The worst candidate, in my opinion, is someone who responds to an ad. You have to screen too many candidates to find a good one because so many of them are unqualified."

Tips From Successful Ad Users

- It's usually best to run display ads, not the smaller classified ads, in the Sales Help Wanted sections of Sunday newspapers. This is the time and place where available salespeople will be looking. The exception might be to run an ad on the travel pages for travel salespeople, sports pages to locate possible sales reps for sporting goods, and so on. These ads are usually more expensive.

• Give your company's name instead of running a blind ad with a box number. The successful salesperson you are seeking will be reluctant to answer a blind ad. Even the line "Our employees know of this ad" does not convince the candidate that the ad might not be run by his own company, a competitor, a major customer, or some other embarrassing prospective employer.

• Sell the benefits of working for your company just as effectively as you want this new sales rep to sell the benefits of your product or service, but don't overpromise—that's a sure way to increase turnover after the new reps have been hired.

• Give a phone number that an interested prospect can call right now, Sunday afternoon, before the impulse passes.

• Tim Duncan of American Greetings adds: "To be successful you must catch the candidate's eye and attract people to your ad. Work with the ad department at the newspaper to incorporate your logo and to use special treatment like borders and bullets. The size of the ad is also important. Larger ones are more expensive, but responses from previous ads may show this to be a worthwhile expense.

"Be sure to list the times and days when calls can be made to you by a potential candidate. Calling times should be convenient for both you and them. Evenings and weekend are preferable when possible.

"The most important aspect of newspaper ads is not to use the ad to do the screening for you, and don't oversell—or *undersell*—the position."

Employment Agencies and Head Hunters

"To use these sources successfully," says Craig Hattabaugh of Aspen Technology, "you need to develop a long-term relationship with them in the same way you would with any other important supplier. Avoid the fly-by-nights."

"When you go to any agency, interview them just as you would a candidate for the job," advises Jack Woods of United States Cellular. "Provide them with a very precise definition of what you want so they can work more intelligently on your behalf. In the long run it will save you time and money."

Tim Duncan of American Greetings says, "I have never been successful in using an agency or head hunter. It has always been a costly waste of time for me. The usual fee of $3,000 to $6,000 to find an entry-level candidate is high and usually unsuccessful. For an agency to find the type of candidate we are seeking, they need to oversell the position and a short time later we lose a disenchanted trainee and gain more downtime in the territory."

Managers who occasionally use agencies successfully say: "Give the agency your job description and person profile. Tell them that the minute they send over an applicant who doesn't meet your minimum specifications, they're through. Screening applicants is what they're getting paid for; don't let them dump the job back in your lap."

Hiring Competitors' Salespeople

Opinion is divided as to the value of this source.

"When you pirate from a competitor," one manager said, "you think you'll be getting a trained salesperson who knows your industry and has important contacts. But sometimes you'll get a misfit, and it's usually more difficult to 'untrain' somebody's unwanted habits than it is to train a rookie from scratch."

Says Tim Duncan of American Greetings: "This never works, and it would take a rare exception for us to even consider it. When I've tried it, I have either gotten someone who has been improperly trained, too set in their ways ('This is how we used to do things') or they've received poor direction from the start and it's too late to turn them around."

But many managers disagree. Typical comments on this side of the issue:

Rob McCoy, GTE:

Sales managers who know their territories also know their competitors and who their best salespeople are. If you recruit from competitors, recruit their best salespeople. You need to be willing to pay for talent. If you offer the low-to-middle range of pay for the open position, you are unlikely to get the talent you want.

Craig Hattabaugh, Aspen Technology:

If you can screen out unsuitable candidates who answer an ad, you should be able to screen out incompetents who are working for a competitor. Also, salespeople experienced in your industry will be able to give as references people you probably already know. Make sure you follow through and question the references.

Tom Dunning, Datacard Corp.:

Our best recruits come from competitors. Selling is the same no matter what the product is, technical or not. You're helping to fulfill people's needs. But in our field, product knowledge is very technical so it makes sense to hire someone who already has it.

Andy Anderson, G. D. Searle:

We spend a lot of time talking with physicians, pharmacists, and drug wholesalers about who are the people—primarily the sales reps of our competitors—who distinguish themselves. We look for a high-profile rep working for a low-profile company. XYZ Co., for example, is not perceived as a very progressive company in the pharmaceutical business. If the physician or pharmacist or wholesaler starts talking about an XYZ sales rep, you know he's a dandy because he distinguishes himself while working for a low-profile company.

Other Sources

"Don't restrict yourself to the traditional sources in recruiting," advises Jack Woods of United States Cellular. "Ask around, talk to other sales managers in your business community, and find out where they have found their people."

Worth contacting are:

1. Sales and marketing executive clubs in your area. Some of them have employment assistance programs for their members.
2. Sales training schools, such as the Dale Carnegie course. Ask the instructor to send you any outstanding enrollees. The school will be glad to cooperate, because it's important to them to be able to say that they can find good positions for qualified candidates.
3. From Lori Schweitzer-Teismann of Olsten Temporaries: "We have pulled in some of our best candidates by getting word of the job opening to professional organizations in which we are represented. We do this by means of an announcement at a monthly meeting or a notice in the organization's newsletter."

Recruiting in Network Marketing

Managers in highly technical fields have to look for the one person in hundreds who can succeed in their type of selling, but managers such as Stan Evans and Ruth Evans, independent distributors of Amway products, have the task of recruiting distributors who will recruit more distributors who in turn will recruit more ad infinitum.

"Most recruits come from referrals," says Stan Evans. "You ask somebody to give you the names of ten people they respect, then contact them with the 'mutual acquaintance' approach. The advantages we can offer the prospective distributor is to be in business for him- or herself without having to invest a lot of capital.

"The person who really succeeds in this business is the one who, after going through friends and relatives and neighbors, begins to find his or her own recruits. That's the real challenge.

"If the person approaches a prospective recruit who's not interested, he or she gets referrals. Sometimes the distributor can offer a little reward for referral names, like a box of candy or something. Sometimes he or she can get the cooperation of somebody like an insurance agent, who's in touch with a lot of people, to furnish leads."

3

Selecting New Sales Representatives

If thousands of dollars will be spent in training a new sales rep, every conceivable method should be used to identify the sales applicants most likely to succeed.

This is not the case with companies selling direct to consumers, who are generally happy to give every applicant a chance. As Amway distributor Stan Evans explains, "We don't try to prejudge people. We want to give everyone a chance. We want them to be presentable, but that doesn't mean they have to wear a coat and tie—in some places that would be laughed at. They have to be presentable according to the customs of their community."

But when it's crucial to pick the best candidate, every first-line sales manager longs for some system that will unerringly select the best sales rep from a group of candidates. And every district manager has long ago learned that there just "ain't no such system." By conscientiously applying every step of a well-planned selection procedure, the manager merely increases the probability that he or she has made the right choice.

Basic Steps in the Selection Process

The basic steps in most selection procedures are:

1. An initial interview
2. Analysis of an application form

3. A more in-depth interview, often with more than one manager interviewing the applicant
4. Aptitude, intelligence, or other tests, if needed
5. A check of the applicant's previous employers and other references, ideally including customers
6. The hiring interview

The screening process need not always be applied rigidly, as illustrated by this experience of Dan Schnaars, president of Flexcon and Systems, Inc. "Recently we have begun to hire on a more planned basis than before. Formerly, I personally interviewed two or three candidates and selected one on the basis of gut feelings. While this method was somewhat successful, it needed improvement.

"Now we run ads and contact employment agencies to bring in a selection of about twenty people. I interview each one, rating them on attitude, aggressiveness, appearance, background, etc. I narrow them down to five finalists, whom we bring in for depth interviews with the general manager and plant manager as well as myself.

"One time when we went through this process, we easily narrowed the field to three candidates. Then we were stalemated. Each of us found something objectionable or questionable about each candidate. We could not pick one with whom we all felt comfortable. As president of the company, I might have broken the deadlock and settled on my preferred candidate.

"Fortunately, my general manager, Danny DuBose, raised the possibility that the *right* person wasn't in this group of three. So, I reviewed my notes on the first interviews and turned up another possibility. He was brought in and found acceptable to all three final interviewers, and he was hired.

"The key was not to feel that the final group of candidates *had* to contain the right choice and to combine the talents of my top two managers with my own. As a result of these two simple ideas, we were able to make an excellent choice."

Another comment on the selection process in general comes from Alex Jones of Allstate Insurance. "The one key characteristic to look for in selecting new salespeople," he notes, "is aggressive career goals both for the immediate and the distant future. If the candidate does not want to earn large amounts of compensation, or develop an exceptionally high living standard, there will be no way for the manager to motivate the new hire to become extremely productive. Motivation comes from within."

"The makeup you look for in individuals to bring into your team must include their ability to work well in a team context," adds Jack

Woods of United States Cellular. "You may bring in a 'hot runner' who overperforms in his own assignment but reduces team productivity. This sacrifices the many for the few."

Similarly, Dave Singer of Cellular One adds: "Don't think of this as just getting another body. Consider the chemistry of your team. Have others on your team meet the candidates. Consider the consequences of your hiring as being similar to a marriage."

Now for a look at the selection process itself.

The Initial Interview

The structure of the initial interview varies. If the candidate has not been previously screened by phone, one purpose of this interview is to find out whether he or she meets the minimum requirements listed in the Person Profile. If, for example, the job requires previous sales experience, a valid driver's license, and the ability to speak Spanish, applicants who don't meet those requirements are quickly but politely told that they don't qualify for the job.

This initial interview gives the manager an opportunity to size up the applicant, ask for and discuss the applicant's resume, determine whether he or she is worthy of further consideration, and, if so, to give the candidate the company's application form.

The screening interview is often conducted by telephone. Some companies run help wanted ads in Sunday newspapers with a phone number the reader can call right then, Sunday morning, to learn more about the job. Those with the minimum qualifications are asked to visit the manager's office or home during the next week.

What do managers look for during this screening interview?

"I look for both the rudimentary qualification and a personality fit," says Craig Hattabaugh of Aspen Technology.

"I look at the grades, of course," says Kevin Flagel of Monsanto Agricultural Company, "but beyond that I look at the individual. Did he work his way through college or did Dad pay for it? I also look for the type of person that will fit into our organization. He or she should be able to meet people—I like them to have a little 'street smarts.' We sell agricultural products through distributors who sell to retailers who sell to farmers. The rep will run into all kinds of people and had better be able to handle them."

Charles Williamson of Nabisco Foods Group comments that "sales managers usually look for bright, personable interns, but sometimes people who are somewhat shy make excellent sales reps."

Screening questions used by Bill Hammick of McKesson Drug include:

- How do you define the word *follow-up*?
- Why do you like people?
- Whom do you most respect?

He also feels it important to let the candidate know that he or she might have to relocate at the end of the training period.

"Another approach to the screening process that can be quite effective," suggests Tim Duncan of American Greetings, "is to run an ad asking for resumes to be sent to you by a target date. By analyzing the resumes, you learn a great deal about the candidates. It enables you to ask specific questions about the individual during the telephone interview. This method allows the interviewer a great deal of flexibility in choosing the interview time and holds an element of surprise to the candidate so that you may be able to learn more about him or her.

"I once ran an ad of this type and received approximately 150 resumes. After analyzing each one, I was able to narrow the field down to the best twelve. This process was not too difficult, as certain knockout factors appeared on many resumes and I could learn more about some candidates from their covering letter.

"I telephoned the twelve individuals, asking questions that had arisen while going over their resumes. I questioned some of the facts given in the resumes and was surprised at the amount of fabricated information. It seems that some of the candidates were unable to read from their resume in front of them and were forced to remember what they had written. Through the telephone interview, I was able to refine the number to four candidates for personal interviews."

Merrill Lynch uses an elaborate form of role-playing as a screening device, says David A. Ruckman, manager of their Cleveland office.

"We can't use psychological examinations because the Equal Employment Opportunity office tells us we don't have sufficient validation. But we do give candidates an exam that tells us whether they are technically able to pass the necessary exams to qualify as a Registered Representative. The test is mainly mathematical; it's one we've developed and used for more than twenty years.

"The second screening is a simulation exercise. After an initial screening of basic ability, we let the candidates 'play broker' for four or five hours in the evening. We simulate the market and have people phone in, playing the roles of clients and prospects. The reactions of the sales applicants are measured by three experienced brokers under the guidance of an expert from our personnel department. How do they handle themselves? Are they ethical? Are they aggressive? The exercise runs from 5:30 to 9:30 p.m., but the four evaluators often discuss the candidates until one o'clock in the morning."

NCR does both the screening and final selection at the same time, as described later under The In-depth Interview.

The Application Form

A good application form is indispensable (see Figure 3-1). The manager analyzes it carefully before the second interview with the applicant, noting any ambiguous details about which to question the candidate.

Things to look for on the application form include:

- Education, if that is a prerequisite.
- General neatness and accuracy in filling out the form. But "be lenient with college students," one manager commented.
- Evidence of excessive "job jumping." If the applicant has switched jobs every year or two in the past, how long will he or she be likely to remain with your company? Craig Hattabaugh points out that the reasons for leaving are more important than the dates.
- Gaps in the employment record. These are sometimes difficult to spot. Jot down the starting and ending dates of each previous position listed and see if there are any time periods not accounted for. If so, you'll want to ask the applicant about this—he or she may have been in jail at the time.
- Long periods of time on the same job, without advancement.

"Any change in the applicant's life may be either a good or bad signal," suggests Don House of NCR. "A person who has gotten out of college, gets married, and takes on some financial responsibility may now have the incentive to become an inspired and dedicated salesperson. But a change can also work in reverse. A person who has been a good, stable producer may go through a divorce or encounter some personal situation that could drastically change incentives and work habits."

The In-Depth Interview

Effective interviewing is difficult for many sales managers, largely because all their previous experience has trained them to talk, and good interviewing requires that they spend most of the time listening. It's not unusual for a manager to spend so much time telling a candidate about the job and the company that at the end of the interview the manager doesn't know much more about the candidate than at the beginning.

The application form can serve as the outline for the interview. For

Figure 3-1. Sample job application form.

		TYPE OF WORK DESIRED	☐ FULL-TIME ☐ SUMMER/INTERN	☐ TEMPORARY/PART-TIME ☐ COOPERATIVE EDUCATION

DOW *Dow U.S.A.*

DATE THIS FORM COMPLETED

PERSONAL

NAME (Last) (First) (Middle)	SOCIAL SECURITY NO
PRESENT ADDRESS (street, city, state, zip code)	AREA CODE & TELEPHONE NO.
PERMANENT ADDRESS, IF DIFFERENT (street, city, state, zip code)	AREA CODE & TELEPHONE NO.

DO YOU HAVE A VALID AUTOMOTIVE OPERATORS LICENSE ☐ YES ☐ NO	DATE AVAILABLE FOR EMPLOYMENT	DID A DOW RECRUITER INTERVIEW YOU? ☐ YES ☐ NO	WHERE/WHEN

ONLY U.S. CITIZENS, ALIENS WHO HAVE A LEGAL RIGHT TO WORK AND REMAIN PERMANENTLY IN THE U.S. OR ALIENS WHO QUALIFY AS "INTENDING CITIZENS" UNDER THE IMMIGRATION REFORM AND CONTROL ACT OF 1986 ARE ELIGIBLE FOR EMPLOYMENT.	ARE YOU A CITIZEN OF THE UNITED STATES? ☐ YES ☐ NO	IF "NO" WHAT IS YOUR VISA CATEGORY STATUS	ALIEN REGISTRATION NUMBER

WORK INTEREST

DESCRIBE THE TYPE OF WORK YOU PREFER AS MUCH DEFINITION AS POSSIBLE WILL BE HELPFUL

LIST ANY STRONG GEOGRAPHIC PREFERENCES ☐ NO PREFERENCE	AREAS OF PREFERENCE	AREAS YOU WOULD NOT CONSIDER	ARE YOU WILLING TO TRAVEL?

EDUCATION

LIST IN CHRONOLOGICAL ORDER THE NAMES OF HIGH SCHOOLS AND COLLEGES ATTENDED	FROM (Mo. & Yr.)	TO (Mo. & Yr.)	DATE DEGREE EARNED OR EXPECTED	DEGREE LEVEL	ACADEMIC MAJOR	GRADE POINT AVERAGE (EX. 2.8/4.0)
HIGH SCHOOL			RECEIVED DIPLOMA YES ☐ NO ☐			
COLLEGES						

THESIS OR ACADEMIC RESEARCH SUBJECT, AND MAJOR PROFESSOR

List any college or academic honors, scholarships or fellowships received (You need not include information indicative of age, sex, religion, race, color, national origin, ancestry or handicap).

IMPORTANT: ATTACH AN OFFICIAL OR UNOFFICIAL COPY OF YOUR TRANSCRIPT(S)

WORK EXPERIENCE

EMPLOYMENT AND BUSINESS EXPERIENCES (Include Permanent, Part-time, Cooperative, Summer and any prior U.S. Military Services)

ORGANIZATION NAME AND ADDRESS, MOST RECENT EMPLOYER FIRST, INCLUDE CITY AND STATE	HOURS/WEEK	FROM (Mo. & Yr.)	TO (Mo. & Yr.)	MONTHLY EARNINGS	NATURE OF WORK AND NAME OF IMMEDIATE SUPERVISOR	REASON FOR LEAVING

MAY WE CONTACT YOUR PRESENT EMPLOYER? ☐ YES ☐ NO

SALARY REQUIREMENTS PER MONTH RANGE [$] - [$]	The law prohibits discrimination against an individual because of age, sex, religion, race, color, national origin, ancestry or handicap. Any item on this form you feel tends to violate Federal or State civil rights legislation need not be completed.

FORM NO. C-26100 PRINTED (REV. 4/91) **DOW IS AN EQUAL OPPORTUNITY EMPLOYER** RBF, INC R-57830

(continued)

Figure 3-1. *Continued.*

ACTIVITIES	**CAMPUS AND/OR PROFESSIONAL AND COMMUNITY ACTIVITIES**			
	Name of Organization and offices held -(You need not list organizations the name or character of which indicates the race, color, religion, national origin, ancestry or handicap of its members)			

		LIST THREE REFERENCES NOT RELATED TO YOU		YEARS KNOWN
REFERENCES	NAME	OCCUPATION OR TITLE	FIRM NAME AND ADDRESS	

OTHER	PLEASE LIST ANY INFORMATION WHICH YOU FEEL PERTINENT TO YOUR DESIRED POSITION	

If you are a Vietnam era veteran, a disabled veteran, or a handicapped individual, you may VOLUNTARILY provide this information. If you provide this information you will be considered under our affirmative action program.

_____

_____

Have you been convicted of a felony crime or released from prison in the past ten years?　☐ YES　☐ NO
Do not include arrests without convictions, misdemeanors, or minor traffic violations.
NOTE: A yes answer does not automatically disqualify you from employment since the nature of the offense, date of the offense, and type of job for which you are applying will be considered.
If yes, please explain (including when, where and disposition of offense): _____

_____

Please read the following statement carefully. Sign only after the entire application has been completed and checked for accuracy.

1. I understand and agree that:

   A . A medical examination and substance abuse screening is required and employment is contingent upon successful completion of the examinations. The results will be held in strict confidence by Dow Medical and Personnel Departments except where release is required by law.

   B . At initial employment I will be expected to sign an Employee Trade Secrets and Patents Agreement. The agreement sets forth the conditions under which The Dow Chemical Company is assigned the entire right, title and interest to any inventions and discoveries made while in Dow's employ. It commits the employee not to divulge to anyone or use, either during or after employment, any trade secret or confidential technical or business information of Dow, other than required in duties while employed by Dow. It commits the employee not to compete in certain areas following termination of employment with Dow. The agreement also protects any previous employer or third party from disclosure of technical or business information that may have been acquired illegally or with restrictions as to secrecy and confirms the "at will" nature of Dow employment.

2. I authorize all persons listed in the Reference Section, schools, current employer(s) (if previously approved by me in the experience section) and all other former employers or organizations listed in this application to provide to Dow any pertinent information requested to arrive at an employment decision.

3. I certify that all information included in this application is accurate to the best of my knowledge and understand that Dow reserves the right to use this information in a background investigation which is required of all employees. I also understand that any misrepresentation or deliberate omission of a fact in my application is justification for refusal of, or if employed, separation from Dow employment.

4. I understand that this employment application and any other Company documents are not contracts of employment and that any individual who is hired may voluntarily leave employment upon proper notice and may be terminated by the Company at any time with or without cause. I understand that no representatives of the Company, other than the Vice President of Human Resources, has any authority to offer or to enter into any agreement for employment for any specified period of time, or to make any agreement contrary to the foregoing.

SIGNED	SIGNATURE OF APPLICANT	DATE

♻ **Printed on recycled paper**

each previous job listed, ask the applicant open-ended questions. "What did you like the most about that job? The least? What was your most important accomplishment? Why did you leave that position?" Other useful questions are: "In what way do you think you could be valuable to my company? Where do you want to be five years from today?" And, of course, this is the time to clarify any questions raised by the study of the application form.

More experienced interviewers will go beyond the commonplace questions suggested above. "They're almost cliches," says Craig Hattabaugh of Aspen Technology, "and the usual answers are worse. Pry deeper. You want to understand this person and what makes him or her tick. What you really need to know is the candidate's motivations and direction. Overlay this on your company's career paths and then ask more specific questions to get more meaningful answers."

Don't misrepresent or oversell the job. One study of new sales hires who quit before the end of their first year revealed that more than half of them left "because the job was misrepresented to me." In view of the fact that it costs many thousands of dollars to hire and train a new sales rep, it's usually better to have an applicant turn down the job than to lure him or her on board by painting too rosy a picture.

"It's extremely important, after developing the applicant's interest in your company's program, to be completely factual in presenting your organization's program to the applicant. It's always wise to present the disadvantages as well as the advantages before a decision is made. This will reduce turnover after the new person is hired. If the tough aspects of the job have been explained, that will eliminate dissatisfaction when they arise."

"Because applicants tend to hear what they want to hear, we give them a written summary of salary structure, expense reimbursements, and other benefits," says Lori Schweitzer-Teismann of Olsten Temporaries in Cincinnati.

One of the most important aspects of the interview is the type of question asked by the recruiter. Some managers follow carefully structured company procedures; others have developed their own favorite questions. Some ideas on this topic follow.

"When asking questions," advises Tim Duncan of American Greetings, "there is one basic rule to follow: If it doesn't pertain to the job, don't ask it!

"A good question is to ask the applicant about the most difficult decision he or she ever had to make. You can see how well they react to pressure and may learn something about their decision-making ability.

"Also ask them to describe their previous (or present) supervisor and peers. Ask, then, how their supervisor and peers would describe the applicant to you. It is also interesting to ask them what qualities they feel a good supervisor should have, and what qualities are essential for the applicant to succeed in the prospective new job. These questions all point to their interpersonal skills, and this may be important in their future position with you.

"Two other good questions are: 'Who is responsible for the greatest success in your life?' and 'Who is responsible for your biggest failure?' You can see whether they place blame or accept responsibility.

"Always end the interview by asking, 'Is there any additional information I did not ask that may assist me in deciding whether to hire you?' And finally, out of courtesy, tell them your time frame in making the decision. And don't forget to take notes."

"NCR does both the screening and the final selection in one interview," reports Patrick Murphy. "Ninety percent of our new sales hires result from college recruiting. Selection is based on a 'target selection' program in which NCR recruiters have been trained. It's a very structured interview procedure in which each applicant undergoes a 45-minute interview by three successive recruiters. They ask general questions, such as 'Tell me about the most recent situation in which you felt a lot of stress.' The candidate's response is graded by the STAR system: situation, task, action, and result. The procedure defines behavioral characteristics.

"After the three recruiters have held 45-minute interviews with each candidate, they compare notes as to candidates' soundness, consistency, and characteristics, and decide right then and there whether to offer a job. It has been quite successful."

Lori Schweitzer-Teismann of Olsten Temporaries finds that she learns a lot about the applicant by simply asking, "Tell me a little about yourself."

"There must be the right 'chemistry' between the manager and the rep," says Tom Dunning of Datacard Corp., "but that doesn't mean hiring people just like you. Other people have skills that can complement your skills. If you're a smiling backslapper, please don't hire all smiling backslappers because that isn't going to work. Hire different kinds of people as long as the chemistry is there."

Be careful not to ask questions that might tempt an unsuccessful candidate to sue you on the grounds that you discriminated against the candidate for reasons of race, color, religion, sex, or national origin. It is also illegal to discriminate, for reasons of age, against anyone between 40 and 70 years old.

Do not ask questions about religion, home ownership, marital status, or family. These regulations may appear to handicap you in your interviewing, but actually they don't. What's important is how the applicant performed in previous jobs and how he or she might perform in yours, and you can ask all the questions you wish along those lines.

If in doubt about any of these fair labor practices guidelines, ask your state Department of Labor for a summary of state laws, or write to the U.S. Department of Labor, Employment Standards Administration, 200 Constitution Avenue, Washington DC 20210.

"After the interview has concluded," advises Tim Duncan of American Greetings, "take time to rate the candidate. This is a good time to reflect on the interview and write your thoughts on paper.

"When all the interviews have been completed, rank the applicants. It is usually difficult to choose between the first and second. If this occurs, go back through your notes, look at your past interview ratings, and make a decision. If it is still too close to call, ask them each back one more time. Explain that you have a difficult decision and again ask what they can do for your company.

"Then weigh their answers. If it's still too close, examine their backgrounds and determine which candidate has the most to gain from the new position; hire that one.

"After you have made your choice, send a letter of appreciation to all the unsuccessful candidates, explaining that they have not been chosen."

Aptitude and Other Tests

Some companies swear by aptitude tests; others won't touch them. If you do plan to use some form of test, follow these suggestions.

1. Be sure it is job-related and not discriminatory.
2. "Validate" the test by giving it to your existing sales force. Compare the test scores of your best and poorest salespeople to see if there is a correlation.
3. Even if you do find a positive correlation, don't rely too heavily on test scores. It's easy to make an arithmetic decision based on scores; it's more difficult, but more effective, to give equal or greater weight to unmeasurable factors such as your impression during the interviews and the comments of previous employers.

A relatively new selection device is the values test. A candidate is likely to perform well at tasks upon which he or she sets a high value. For example, a person who believes that planning is valuable is likely to be a good planner. Values Research Group uses a values scan developed by Robert S. Hartman to develop a values profile of an individual. This is compared with similar profiles of four successful employees.

"Don't place too great a value on the results of tests," cautions Tim Duncan of American Greetings. "Some people who are great achievers test poorly, and many underachievers test well. Use the test as an equal variable in your equation along with their experience, performance in previous jobs, and results of the interview."

One nonbeliever in tests is Bill Nyberg of United Homecraft in St. Louis. "I used to use tests but discontinued it because I found that if the applicant sells me on himself or herself, I have a good sales rep.

"I ask a lot of questions like 'Why do you want to work here? Why should I consider you for this position? What will your wife or husband think of what you're doing? How much money do you want to make?' If the answer is '$25,000,' I'm not interested."

Previous Employment Check

Two sources of information about the applicant are previous employers and the references listed on the application form. Employers are a more important source because no one will list a reference who will give derogatory information.

There's probably no better indicator of how an applicant will perform on your job than how that applicant performed on previous jobs. This means that a careful check of previous employers is a must— and an increasingly difficult must.

It's a waste of time to check references by mail. Employers are reluctant to put negative comments in writing for fear of being sued. So check references in person or by phone, and even here you'll find that an increasing number of companies will refuse to give any information at all.

In making a phone check, explain to the former employer, "X, who used to work for you, is applying for a position with us, and I'd appreciate it if you'd just verify what he/she said about the position and salary." This seems like a reasonable request, and after you have obtained that information you can try continuing with such questions as: "What sort of work did he or she do?" "How well did he or she get along with superiors or with other employees?" "What were his or her greatest strengths or accomplishments?" "Do you know of any weaknesses or handicaps that would interfere with a career in our company?" "If the individual applied to be reinstated, would you rehire him or her?"

Lori Schweitzer-Teismann of Olsten Temporaries says that "we need team players, not individual virtuosi. Therefore, we ask references or previous employers, 'Was the candidate a joiner or a one-man band?

Did the candidate trust the inside staff or insist on handling the order from start to finish?' "

"Checking previous employers is extremely difficult," adds Tim Duncan of American Greetings. "Most previous employers will give only positions held and dates employed. You can usually get a position description from the employer, and this may loosen them up to discuss more with you. After asking the usual questions you've listed in advance, end the conversation by asking, 'Is there anything else you can tell me about this person?' You may get lucky!"

"In today's environment," adds the Communications Sales Manager, "it is imperative to do a thorough background check for any litigation, pending lawsuits, previous judgments, and such. Also, check with the named educational institutions to validate stated achievements.

"Another possibility is to ask if the candidate's previous work has involved contacts with some of your customers or clients. If so, ask them about their experiences with the candidate."

"Have the candidate interviewed by one or two others in a nonselling capacity in the office," recommends Jack Woods of United States Cellular. "This will provide you with extra sets of eyes. For example, have the candidates meet with the accounting people. Since the new trainee will be interacting with these people, it's good to get their perspective on the candidate before making your decision."

The Hiring Interview

Since there has been so much careful screening and two-way communication before this step, the hiring interview tends to be a formality.

Compensation and fringe benefits are explained in detail, information needed for the company's health care program is obtained, contracts and receipts for autos or equipment are signed, and the new hire is introduced to—and welcomed by—company executives.

Specific Selection Procedures

Some participants provided detailed descriptions of their companies' selection procedures. Following are their comments.

R. S. Layman, NCR:

We hire sales trainees right out of college rather than hiring experienced salespeople. We try to hire the cream of the college crop. We look at grade point averages, technical degrees, strength in verbal communications. We screen candidates at colleges and invite selected applicants to Saturday interviews at one of the seven divisional headquarters.

Each candidate is interviewed separately by three district sales managers, who follow a structured outline for a one-hour interview (the three outlines differ). They look for past accomplishments rather than asking what the candidate would do in some future hypothetical situation. Not a "what would you do?" but a "what *did* you do?" question. We call it the STAR approach: identify Situation or Task, Action taken, and Results. We go for very specific things they did as individuals, not what a team did.

At the end of the interview, the managers can ask their own questions or engage candidates in a general conversation. Each DM interviews three candidates in the morning and three in the afternoon. Each DM rates each candidate, then the three arrive at a consensus rating for each: hire, reject, or reinterview. The use of three different interviewers eliminates any "halo effect" or prejudice one interviewer might have.

As for general recommendations to interviewers, be very careful not to inject your own bias. I feel that each applicant should be interviewed by three to five persons.

Andy Anderson, G. D. Searle:

Before we hire anyone, after the first interview with the first-line manager, we like to have the prospect work two days in the field with a representative to make sure they understand and like the climate in which they will be working. I want the prospective new hire to hear, from a rep in the first-line manager's district, what the job is like. By the second day all barriers are down; we think that's important.

After the fieldwork, there's a second interview with the district manager, where the potential new rep will have some very specific questions to ask. Then there's a third interview with the regional manager. And, of course, the opinion of the rep with whom the new person has worked is highly valued.

Alex Jones, Allstate Insurance:

I used to think I could judge people based on my impressions of them, but it didn't take me many years to figure out that's not a very good way to hire people.

We have a set of guidelines. We're looking for people with college degrees, a background we can track on paper and verify.

I don't do any gut hiring anymore. Some fellow will walk in and tell me he's the greatest in the world, suede-shoe type with all the answers, but when you dig into his background, he's been a floater with five companies in the past five years. Nothing is going to make him change.

So what we look for is trackable evidence of success patterns in the person's background: with one employer for two and one-half or three years, been promoted or received a raise, had evidence we can look at.

When being interviewed for a job, the applicant is going to tell you everything you want to hear. In the past I've hired such people, and that's the last time you see any evidence of what they have done. They come to work late, leave early, goof off, and if you go back and look at the original application, you ask yourself why in the world you ever hired this person. The weaknesses are as plain as the nose on your face.

At Allstate we use a computer tracking system to evaluate the applicant's background. An outside vender called TRACOM developed it for us. We give applicants a questionnaire about their backgrounds, education, home ownership or rental, previous jobs, salary or commission, promotions, hobbies—280 questions. Over a four-year period we tracked all new hires, compared their degree of success with their answers on the questionnaire to identify the predictors. We divided them into four categories: superior, above average, average, and below average performers. From this they built the computer scoring system, which now uses only about fifty questions. Applicants can enter their own answers into the computer, and we forward the information to the test center by phone. We hire only from the top two categories.

Bob Higham, CIBA:

We use the Targeted Selection Criteria process and it has worked out very well—for me, at least. This starts with a half-hour to 45-minute screening interview based on the applicant's resume. If it is a go situation, the next step is an interview of approximately two hours by the hiring district manager. The manager is looking for a number of things:

- The applicant's ability to learn the technical language that is necessary in our field
- Sales and/or communication skills
- Sales ability and persuasiveness
- Oral communication skills
- Initiative and work standards (which can be picked up from the applicant's work history or college record)
- The applicant's impact on the district manager

* The applicant's sensitivity to the needs of others, specifically customers
* Tenacity, resilience, and—very important—planning and organizing abilities
* Problem-solving ability

If it is still a go situation, a second district manager is called in to do a similar in-depth interview.

At each stage of this process, the applicant is given a role-playing situation. One of them is a sales presentation, another involves problem solving or a customer complaint, the third involves planning.

If the applicant still looks desirable, there is a third in-depth interview by the next level of management. The three managers then compare their impressions. This system has worked quite well, because what one manager may miss, another may readily pick up, based on the different questions the individual managers have developed.

In the interviewing process I am not interested in hearing from the applicant what "we" did; what I am interested in is what the individual applicant did on his own or her own.

Charles Williamson, Nabisco Foods Group:

Topnotch sales reps are hard to find, especially those just starting their careers. There are several steps I use to find good-quality people.

After the initial screening interview, I arrange for the applicant to spend one to two hours with one of our better sales reps. The results are threefold: first, the applicant has the opportunity to observe the job firsthand; second, the applicant can ask questions and get answers from a prospective peer; third, the sales rep may observe and ask questions of the applicant in a natural, on-the-job setting.

The sales rep then reports his or her observations and opinions to me. The applicant also reports back as to continued interest in the job. (On several occasions, the applicant has never been heard from again.) This procedure also eliminates any possible misrepresentation of the job. This method has produced my best and most productive employees.

Families of prospective employees are also important. Untidy spouses, untidy automobiles—those filled with litter—usually indicate a person who is not neat, accurate, or timely.

Having lunch with an applicant with the spouse present can be an eye-opener or an indication of the support so necessary to most sales positions.

Our sales job at Nabisco involves physically stocking shelves and building displays. Applicants who are involved in strenuous hobbies or sports have a better chance of surviving the rigors of the sales/service position.

A good sales rep must be a good communicator. Discussing the job and asking questions during an interview will usually get a lot of stock answers—answers the applicant has memorized. This does not necessarily indicate that the applicant is a good communicator or is able to sell to customers.

We use the "front porch" method of evaluating their communicative abilities. This requires setting up a casual meeting somewhere neutral, such as in a park, a family-type restaurant at a slow time, or your own front porch, if you have one. It is amazing how much more a person will open up in a casual setting.

Questions about family and friends, school activities, their feelings on some local issue, and so on will lead to an informal discussion. A candidate who answers with only yes, no, or very short answers, with no self-inspired questions or comments, will usually not be able to get the inside track with a customer and get those big orders.

Howard Strelsin, Terminix International:

We had a psychologist prepare questionnaires that were sent to outstanding performers in our three specialized areas of selling: termite control, pest control, and commercial pest control. Based on the responses, we came up with a profile of what we were looking for in each position as well as a manual describing a focused interviewing technique our managers use. It lists the questions they can ask regarding the skills required and job responsibilities of the particular position. Some applicants are experts at being interviewed.

We are very careful in checking references and previous employers, believing that past behavior is the best predictor of future behavior. We have a checklist the manager uses, with such items as the number of jobs the applicant has held in the last five years, too many yes or no answers (four no answers in any category are a red flag).

Never hire anyone on the first interview. We try to make the second interview at a different time to see if the applicant is willing to come back at 8:00 A.M. or 5:30 P.M. or Saturday morning.

Managers who have the best selection record make the job offer while sitting down with the applicant's spouse. Our jobs require a lot of evening and Saturday work, so we want to make sure the spouse is truly supportive.

We also use aptitude tests for sales reps. Potential management trainees, after several interviews, are flown to Memphis for a half-day of testing at a psychologist's headquarters, using a validated Terminix test battery. The result is an eight- or nine-page report sent to the regional manager under whom the prospective branch manager will be working.

Computer Sales Manager:

I believe in interviewing applicants several times myself, in several different environments—my office, at lunch, over drinks—just to see how they handle themselves. The more I see them, the more I learn. We also have several other managers interview them to get more than one opinion.

We have the candidate spend at least half a day in the field with one of our senior salespeople. The candidate gets a real feel for the job, and our rep feeds back observations on the candidate's energy, enthusiasms, interests, and types of questions asked.

Jim Nichols, Dow Chemical USA:

The application form is critical. A tremendous amount of information can be obtained from it. Education and grade point average in both high school and college are important. Also, depending on the job requirements, you might ask about geographical preferences; assuming you are looking for a seller to be with your company for a long time, you may wish to determine his or her willingness and ability to be transferred geographically.

Also, be clear in describing the travel requirements of the job, such as average nights away from home. Some recruits may be single parents or have some other restriction on their personal time that would prevent them from doing the job properly but might not show up on the application.

The question of money should be addressed up front. What are you willing to pay? What would the employee earn if the job is performed satisfactorily? Give this information on the application so you will know immediately whether you are talking the same language.

The application form should ask for a complete job history, including jobs held while getting an education. This could be an indicator of the recruit's industriousness and determination. Questions about schooling should also cover extracurricular activities.

On interviewing, it is important that candidates be interviewed by four or five different people with diverse interests in the job—for example, the sales manager, personnel manager, headquarters product manager, and an uninvolved sales manager. Also, don't hesitate to get input from the secretary who acts as host in ushering the candidate from one office to the next. The recruit may be more relaxed with that person and expose information not detected in the interview.

Finally, these days, many companies insist on testing for the use of drugs along with routine physicals prior to employment. Take advantage of this possibility. It is one of the few times you may have the opportunity to detect a problem.

4
Initial Training

The role of the first-line manager in breaking in a new sales rep varies widely from company to company. In small companies the first-line manager, who may be the sales manager or even the owner, does all the recruiting and training. Many large corporations provide intensive training at headquarters and deliver ready-made graduates to the field, but even in these cases the role of the first-line manager in orienting and motivating the new hire is important.

Because the first-line manager in any event will be responsible for the new rep's performance, the manager can have a mental or written inventory of what the new seller must know and can fill in any gaps in the headquarters training, or localize it to the specific requirements of the district.

What Every Sales Rep Needs

An inventory of the knowledge and skills required of a new rep includes:

- Product and application knowledge
- Selling skills
- Time and territory management
- Work habits
- Company reports and procedures

To this basic list, the Communications Sales Manager adds, "Knowledge of the company, its history, strengths, organization; knowledge of available support tools, and knowledge about satisfied clients."

Training can be done by a headquarters training department, by the new rep's first-line manager, or by an experienced sales rep. In most companies the training is some combination of these.

Training by the First-Line Manager

Following are suggestions to first-line managers who do most of the training themselves.

R. S. Layman, NCR:

Don't expect too much too fast. Hit a balance between "Watch me do it" and "Now you try it." The important thing is to help the rep develop good habits as early as possible.

Tom Dunning, Datacard Corp.:

You have to spend time with them. There's two ways you can learn the selling aspect of the job: getting thrown out of places, or having your manager coach you, and the second is the most desirable. Headquarters training in sales skills is less effective than field coaching.

Jim Nichols, Dow Chemical USA:

It's very important to develop good habits in the sales rep early on. Traveling with successful, motivated sellers prior to field assignment and regular, close contact with the first-line manager will help the new seller through the little but frequent first-time problems that arise. I like to require call reports on *every* call for three to six months. It gives the manager a view of what the seller is doing on calls and how the seller is thinking about problems. It also alerts the manager to situations that need attention or training.

David A. Ruckman, Merrill Lynch:

Selling brokerage services is full of rejections while prospecting and full of abuse from customers whose investments are going down. Where the sales manager can be most useful is in keeping the rep's morale up, saying "Everything's okay, just keep working at it." Constant encouragement is the key.

Alex Jones, Allstate Insurance:

My primary advice is not to short-change the trainees on the amount of time and attention you give them. There's a tendency, once you get the new rep aboard, not to give him or her high priority. You've made a huge investment in hiring and training the new rep—anywhere from $50,000 to $75,000 to recruit and train these people and keep them on the payroll for a year or two. The important thing is to hire the right person in line with the old cliche about the silk purse and the sow's ear. If you've hired the right person, it makes sense to spend enough time with them up front to get them started right. Show them where they made mistakes so they don't keep doing them over and over. Be available any time they have questions.

Craig Hattabaugh, Aspen Technology:

The first calls for the trainee should be simple ones, like dropping off a new piece of literature, or being introduced as the new rep on the territory. In these simple calls, let the trainee run the show. Don't hesitate to bring the trainee along on more important calls, although naturally the new sales rep's participation will vary inversely with the importance of the call.

As the reps become more experienced and start handling the calls themselves, the manager must resist taking control of the conversation and let trainees develop their own styles—the manager stepping in only when things go bad. Trainees are very impressionable. You don't want them to emulate anyone but themselves.

Jack Woods, United States Cellular:

The manager should have a formal action plan that thoroughly covers the development procedure. It must be elementary and must not leave anything to chance. Two or three months spent up front can pay you ten times over down the road.

Dave Singer, Cellular One:

One of the difficulties is that sales managers can be so busy that they bring in the new hires and let them sit at a desk and fend for themselves. Have a very specific game plan covering the first few weeks for your new hires, detailing how the organization works, whom to go to for answers, and so on. Meet with the new person at the end of each week to review accomplishments and make plans.

Using a Field Guru

If the manager lacks the time to give the necessary training to the new hire, it may be possible to delegate the indoctrination task to an experienced salesperson. The trainee travels with this tutor for days or weeks, until he or she has acquired enough knowledge to start out alone (with some follow-up coaching, of course).

Selection of the field trainer is important. Usually it should not be a superstar, who frequently has developed unorthodox ways of doing things that the fledgling is unable to imitate. The field trainer should receive some compensation for time and effort expended in tutoring the new person—otherwise the procedure may be a mere "tag-along" exercise rather than a real learning experience.

If the trainee can be of great assistance to the experienced seller in setting up displays or exhibits or handling demonstrations, that in itself may be sufficient compensation. If not, it's desirable to offer the trainer a small override on the new person's productivity for the first six months or so. This really motivates the trainer to ensure that the trainee has all the needed knowledge and skills.

Commenting on the use of a seasoned rep to do the training, Kevin A. Flagel of Monsanto Agricultural Co. says: "I'm not so sure the manager is the best person to do the training. We use seasoned sales reps—those who have been around a long time—to break in the new reps, and we compensate them for doing it. I'm traveling all the time, but the senior sales rep is usually home most evenings and has more time for the new person. We've tried it both ways and found that the seasoned sales rep is the best trainer. The new rep gets one county as his or her new territory, and almost every evening or every morning they get together with their trainer.

"The informal field training lasts about three months. We have a checkoff list of about twenty-five items that the field trainer uses as a guide to what must be covered. The product development manager and I have to agree that the trainee knows these topics to qualify the trainee to go to our headquarters in St. Louis for two weeks of formal training."

"I believe in exposing a sales trainee to as many field sales reps as possible," suggests Bill Hammick of McKesson Drug Co. "Everybody does things a little differently, and the trainee can pick up good points from a variety of reps. It's very important to interview the trainees after each field trip to get their impressions of the good techniques they saw. I don't ask about the bad things they saw—for obvious reasons.

"At the end of each week the trainees write individual reports summarizing what they learned during the past week, in what areas they feel they need more exposure, and any suggestions for improving the training."

Training Content

The content of a successful training program should include the following: knowledge of the product, sales skills, management of time and territory, work habits, and company reports and procedures. Following a discussion of each are some tips on successful initial training.

Product Knowledge

The first-line manager who has to impart product knowledge from scratch can usually work from catalogs and price sheets, being careful to give the information in small doses and to get feedback by using questions, quizzes, or assignments to make sure the trainee has assimilated it.

If product knowledge has been imparted in headquarters training, the local management can provide an important supplement by having the trainee visit various types of customers to see the product in use.

Olsten Temporaries of Cincinnati has trainees spend a week sitting in on the interviewing, testing, and placement of temporary employees, as well as the billing procedures. "How could a trainee sell a product without understanding what happens when an order is placed?" asks Lori Schweitzer-Teismann of Olsten.

Sales Skills

The fact that the new salesperson was a successful seller for a previous employer doesn't necessarily mean that he or she has acquired the selling skills needed in the new position.

If sales skill training has not been adequately provided as part of headquarters training, the first-line manager can:

1. "Start with a thorough analysis of your company's selling process," advises Craig Hattabaugh of Aspen Technology. "Too many managers jump into field training before teaching the company's selling strategy and philosophy."
2. Demonstrate the desired sales skills by letting the trainee accompany the manager on sales calls.
3. Let the trainee travel with two or three successful sales reps to see different styles of selling at work.

4. Send the trainee to a sales training course. Instruct the trainee in advance that he or she will be expected to give a subsequent report on how the general principles covered in the sales training course can apply to the particular products, customers, and sales obstacles of the new job.
5. Encourage the trainee to read books on selling.

The topic of field coaching both new and experienced salespeople is so important that it is covered more extensively in Chapter 6.

Time and Territory Management

The ability to manage their time and territories effectively is as important to salespeople as their selling skills.

If the job consists largely of calling on established customers, the manager needs to explain: (1) what kind of customer and prospect records to keep and how to use them, (2) what percentage of time to spend on nonbuying prospects, (3) how sales calls and time should be allocated among product lines and among large, medium, and small customers, and (4) how much time should be allocated to nonselling duties.

"But," cautions Craig Hattabaugh, "this should serve as a starting framework only. Then let the rep manage the territory for a while, check on results, and correct as necessary."

For the one-time sale, such as construction projects, corporate aircraft, pension programs, and so on, the manager can suggest a similar allocation of time among sales functions: prospecting, preparing proposals, follow-up calls, servicing existing customers, and so on.

Work Habits

The first-line manager can be extremely useful to the trainee by suggesting the procedures or habits that generate success. This includes such topics as how and when to plan next week's work and tomorrow's work, the type of planning required for important as well as routine calls, and how to handle call reports, expense accounts, and other paperwork expeditiously.

Company Reports and Procedures

It's interesting to note that sales reps in every type of selling seem to do the same amount of griping about paperwork, whether they're required to submit two reports a week or twenty.

A manager is more likely to get the necessary reports promptly and accurately if he or she explains to the new sales rep how each report is used, why the information is important to the company, and (where applicable) how the sales rep can use his or her copies of the report to improve territory coverage.

Tips on Initial Training

Here are some suggestions by participants on how to set up a successful initial training routine.

Bill Nyberg, United Homecraft:

Unlike some people in the home improvement industry who train only for a day or so, we have an intensive two-week training program. We have separate sales forces for windows, siding, insulation, kitchen, and bathroom.

The training program covers everything from product knowledge, on which we are very strong, to making the sales presentation. We work from 9 A.M. until 10 or 11 P.M., some of it in the classroom but a lot of it out in the field with salespeople.

Howard Strelsin, Terminix International:

We have a structured training program divided into five phases:

1. *A brief orientation phase.* During this phase, trainees are introduced to people in the branch, given a job description and explained what is expected of them, a preview of the next three or four weeks of training, the structure of the organization, and employee benefits.

2. *Field service familiarization.* Because they'll be selling a service, we want them to actually see the services being performed and sometimes, under supervision, performing the services themselves. They actually serve as apprentices for a short period. At the same time they take a two-part home study course: the Key Man course on termite control, and the Anchor Man course on pest control.

3. *The product knowledge phase.* This is technical information on pest problems and their solutions, using interactive video tapes and sessions with the branch manager.

4. *Sales techniques.* These include presentation, objections, probing questions, and closing. The branch manager is ultimately responsible for this training; however, if there is an outstanding salesperson in the

branch, the trainee may ride with him or her for a few days to observe the selling process.

5. *Organization and prospecting*. These include paperwork, how to organize follow-ups, and how to go after business if you don't have a lead. We have fifteen programs that a person can work on, some for short-term results, some over the long term.

The ultimate training responsibility is with the branch manager, who wears several hats—responsibility for service and for branch profitability. He often has a service manager, sometimes an office manager for administrative duties, but rarely a sales manager. Whenever someone else in the branch is assigned a training segment, it is imperative that the manager review with this trainer exactly what the manager wants the trainee to learn. We sometimes take this for granted.

Computer Sales Manager:

When the employee arrives on the job the first day, he or she is given a package of five separate workbooks, along with a training schedule that will take them through the first six weeks on the job. These books all contain product information, and each has a test at the end that must be sent in before the trainee can be sent for corporate training. The recruits work on these books on their own time and can complete them and review them several times before corporate training.

The trainees meanwhile spend the first two weeks going through a fully structured program that allows them to spend time in each department, meeting the various individuals, working in the department, learning what it does. During this orientation they also learn about company benefits, corporate philosophy, and so forth.

After this two-week orientation, trainees spend the next four weeks observing sales calls, attending sales meetings, and reviewing audio and audiovisual training tapes.

After six weeks, trainees go to corporate headquarters for two and one-half weeks of in-depth product and sales training. On the first day of this training, they're given an entrance exam to test their level of preparedness for the classroom training. If any individuals are not prepared and might hold up the rest of the class, they may be sent back to their regions.

Upon returning to their regions after corporate training, they are assigned a territory and begin work. On most of their initial sales calls, they are accompanied by their sales manager who continues their training "on the job." It is not unusual for the sales manager to go on a high percentage of the new person's calls, particularly the big ones, for the first full year of employment.

In our company, sales training is an ongoing process. We hold a one-and-one-half-hour sales training class for all salespeople every Wednesday morning. In addition, several times a year we hold sales training workshops and also continuously distribute sales educational information on a weekly basis.

Bob Higham, CIBA:

Our initial training in products and technical knowledge, with some sales skills training, is done by our training department. When the rep gets out in the field the first day, there is no question in my mind but that the first-line manager should be with that representative for approximately two weeks or ten working days.

The first day is spent on company reports and procedures. For the next nine days it is in the field with the new rep getting his or her feet wet. I usually do the sales presentations for the first couple of days, and then the representative takes over.

It is important that the new representative self-critiques after each call, discussing with the manager the good parts of the call and what could have been done better.

I have on occasion used what I will call a "district trainer"—usually a representative who excels in communication skills—but this has not happened very often, as I am a firm believer that since this new representative is going to be reporting to the district manager, that manager should be with the representative those first two weeks. After these first two weeks, it is time that the representatives get out on their own. Let them start knocking on doors. I think it is also very important that the field manager keep lines of communication open with the representative and get back to working with the rep no later than one month later.

Approximately four to six months later, the rep returns to sales training for a refresher, so to speak, and this gives the reps an opportunity to sharpen their sales skills as well as gain additional technical knowledge. One of the positive aspects of this refresher is that the reps are back with the same group of their peers they started out with.

Jerry McCloskey, Heinz U.S.A.:

Initial training at Heinz is handled by the area manager, who is the first-line supervisor. He will give the new trainee the product manuals, systems and procedures, retail ad function, expense reports, and so on.

During the first day in the field, the manager will do a walk-through of several stores to show the new rep—territory supervisor at Heinz—the general layout and product displays. Then the manager will make a few retail calls as if he were the territory supervisor for those stores, while the trainee observes the objectives, procedures, and strategies of the call.

On the second day the new territory supervisor makes the calls, discussing the procedures with the manager until a smooth flow has been developed. On the third day the rep again observes the manager making calls, and on the fourth day the rep makes calls and the manager critiques.

During the second week the rep makes calls alone, taking notes after each call to discuss with the manager by phone that evening. On the third week the manager observes and critiques the rep's calls.

After a minimum of one year in the territory, the new hires are brought to Pittsburgh headquarters for a week of company orientation, growth opportunities, and a professional selling skills course. Heinz has developed its own retail reporting system called SAS (Sales Achievement System) that alerts the territory supervisor as to what needs to be accomplished with each account and on each call. It is a professional tool for diagnosing problems and pinpointing priorities.

The SAS system works from top to bottom. Monthly goals and achievements are shown by region, district, area, and individual territory. It is used not as a critique, but as a means for pinpointing needs wherever they exist.

Another important step in indoctrinating new hires is to give them an overview of how their work fits into the entire marketing and merchandising plan of the district. Letting them go on a key account call that impacts on their territory and letting them travel with another territory supervisor who is aware of marketing strategies does contribute to their knowledge and know-how.

Before each call, the supervisor should ask the rep what the goal for the call is. Are there real problems to be addressed? Is there a nagging distribution problem? Or a noncommittal manager? These problems require forethought so that some positive step can be achieved on each call.

One old story around Heinz concerns a fairly new rep riding with a veteran supervisor. Before the first call the supervisor asked, "What's important about this store and why are we making this call?" "Nothing special," the rep relied. "Then let's skip this call and go on to the next one."

Before the second call the manager asked the same question and got the same type of response. They skipped that call too. By the time the third call rolled around, the rep caught on and gave a very specific objective for the call and proceded to achieve it.

Charles Williamson, Nabisco Foods Group:

Many outstanding potential recruits are lost during this time period because of improper training and follow-up. Each new employee is different and must be evaluated to ascertain the type, amount, and duration of training needed.

Most new interns have very little idea of "how to sell." Personal selling techniques are not usually taught in college.

A sales manager must never be too busy to listen and coach at a moment's notice. Questions that may seem almost silly should be answered carefully and in depth.

We require new sales reps to keep a notebook on the front seat of the car to record questions after each call. The new rep is usually working with an experienced sales rep, one with patience and good habits.

Some very important facts we tell all new recruits are: "Your training is largely in your own hands. You must force the answers from those you work with until you know everything that is done and how to do it. Bring your questions to sales meetings."

Most first-line managers are not blessed with an entire group of topnotch reps. Usually 20 to 30 percent are producing just enough to get by, and this group is not usually your newest or youngest. If this group is worth saving, then they should be worth motivating to become at least 60 to 70 percent producers.

Careful and considered guidance must be used to make them part of the team. All our great sales reps are or have been part of a support group, which is a small gathering of three or four persons meeting weekly for about an hour and discussing each person's problems and opportunities, feeding on positive thinking concepts as a group. By including poor performers in this group, with proper introduction as to its usefulness, the increased effectiveness of these people is almost phenomenal.

Another method used for this group is to issue challenges that start small and grow as each objective is met. One example would be a challenge to place a reasonable amount of a new product during a four-week period. Setting a goal for a number of new placements with existing customers is another example. We then slowly increase the goals, with proper recognition as each one is met. All tend to build both confidence and effectiveness.

Careful consideration must be given to avoid overdoing the attention to the poor performers as they may use their poor results as an attention-getter.

Once the manager and rep have agreed that the rep has the ability and confidence to set and reach the desired goals, the rep must be cut loose to do just that. Reps must have the freedom to realize the satisfaction of doing it on their own.

Tim Duncan, American Greetings:

At American Greeting we use an elaborate training system for our newly hired sales reps. Since our company has such a diverse range of products and thousands of individual items to learn about, we must take the necessary time to teach them well.

We give the new hire a sixty:forty ratio of actual field time compared with home study time. American Greetings produced its own video self-learning course to expose the sale reps to conditions they might not otherwise experience for some time. The rep watches a section of the video and then reads about what happened in a manual. The rep then takes a short self-scoring quiz on the material. If the rep misses a question, he or she can reread the section and take the quiz again.

Because the manager has a guide to the material studied each night, the lesson the rep studied the night before can be discussed and even applied during the work-with next day. This pattern of reading assignment/video/quiz/field application enables the rep to retain more of the information.

This initial training session lasts for two weeks and is followed by four weeks of actual selling monitored by the district manager. The rep then attends a one-week seminar at headquarters to fine-tune selling skills. After six months in the field, reps return to headquarters for a one-week advanced training seminar.

The most important aspect of our training program is that it is continuous. Our sales reps and managers are trained in some aspect of their jobs on an on-going basis. We feel you can learn something every day if you keep your eyes open, listen, and pay attention.

5

Keeping the
Sales Force Motivated

According to Jerry McCloskey of Heinz U.S.A., "Motivation is the backbone of selling. The best sales managers have a knack of stimulating the creativity of their people. Either collectively or one-on-one, the manager challenges each person's psyche."

It's not easy. If any sales manager, anywhere, has devised some simple method for keeping every member of the sales force highly motivated at all times, that manager has not yet shared the secret with the world. The difficulty is that no two people are motivated in exactly the same way, and within one individual motivations may vary from time to time.

This chapter briefly reviews some of the well-known theories of motivation, then discusses specific applications to the sales force. Two common motivators—incentive compensation and sales contests—are treated in Chapters 14 and 15.

Hiring "Hungry" People

Some people "just naturally" seem to have more built-in drive than others, whether inherited or acquired. Since it's difficult to change the degree of this basic inner motivation, sales managers try to hire reps who are "hungry" to begin with.

During the application interview, experienced sales reps know all the "right" answers to appear highly motivated. Ask them what their career goal is and they'll reply "to get your job" or "to be president of this company."

It's more important to assess their degree of motivation by analyzing applicants' previous behavior. What did they do to earn money while in high school or college? Are they doing anything on a part-time basis to increase their total earnings in their present jobs? What are they doing in the way of self-development to increase their capabilities?

"Aside from earning money in high school and college, the applicant may have been involved in other equally important activities," notes Tim Duncan of American Greetings. "Make sure there was a genuine need to earn money. If not, applicants should have been highly active in extracurricular activities. This indicates a higher desire for self-development, for improvement that leads to leadership and management skills.

"I think I am a good example of this theory. I attended school through a partial sports scholarship, and my parents paid the remainder. This gave me time to participate in student government, preside over the sports committee, write for the student newspaper, perform in school plays, and engage in other activities."

"Motivation is an internal thing," says Alex Jones of Allstate Insurance Co. "You have to hire people who are self-motivated. One of the ways to emphasize their goals is to do a lot of business planning with reps before you hire them. Find out what they hope to accomplish in their first year, their second year, their third year, five years from now, ten years from now, when they retire. If you hire someone who is thirty years old and whose goal is to make $40,000 a year, that person isn't going anywhere."

Basic Theories of Motivation

Every discussion of motivation summarizes the ideas of the leading theorists in the field of motivation: MacDougal, Herzberg, Maslow, Skinner, McClelland. It's interesting to note that the field of selling, where motivation probably has a more direct effect upon productivity than in other types of work, has rarely been studied by specialists in motivation.

Following is a review of the basic theories.

The Hawthorne Effect

In a pioneering study in an electrical manufacturing plant in the 1920s, psychologists isolated one group of women workers and experimented with variations in lighting, rest periods, and other aspects of the environment. No matter what they did, production increased. They

eventually concluded that this group of workers was breaking all production records simply because men with white jackets and clipboards
were paying attention to them. They were the only group in the factory
receiving this attention. They were *important!*

Another study in a New Jersey factory indicated that the one thing
that was most influential in motivating employees was the feeling that
"my boss listens to me." Again, the individual worker was made to feel
important.

This certainly applies in selling. A good first-line manager takes an
interest in each rep—in his or her productivity, progress, family, hobbies, birthdays, goals, problems.

"When the manager spends two or three days in the field with a
sales rep every two months or so," says Tim Duncan, "this makes the
rep feel important. These work-with sessions give the manager a chance
to evaluate reps' needs and determine how best to motivate them.

"Make sure while working with them that you ask the right questions and really listen to the answers. At the end of the work-with
session, write the rep a letter evaluating the last two days and summarizing the topics discussed. This makes the reps feel better about you as
a manager, about the company, and about themselves."

"I've thought a lot about motivation during the last twenty years,"
writes Bill Nyberg of United Homecraft in St. Louis, "and there is a
magic answer. I've used awards like sales trips for the reps and their
spouses—my top rep will make more than $75,000 this year—but the
secret is that I spend time with them, I give them personal attention, I
know their spouses, I know what's bothering them, I spend personal
time with them.

"We have other forms of personal recognition: when they hit a
million dollars in sales, they get a jacket with the company patch on it,
we have a President's Club with a watch awarded for something above
the call of duty, we have a ring program for longevity.

"We do a lot of that type of thing, but I have to tell you that I have
a sliding glass door to my office instead of a wooden one, and it's always
open. We have a rather large sales office and I spend a lot of my time
back there, since about twenty-five reps report to me during the season.
Years ago I probably spent six or eight hours a day on desk work and
two hours with salespeople; today it's probably the opposite. How do
you get the desk work done in two hours? Hire a good secretary to
whom you pay a good salary."

"One of the best ways to motivate people is to take lots of interest
in helping them meet their personal goals," agrees Alex Jones of Allstate
Insurance Co. "You work with them, helping them set goals for one
year ahead, two years, three years. Then you don't let up, you work

with them elbow to elbow to help them reach their goals. At least once a week review their progress toward their goals."

"Communication is all important" is another variation on the same theme, this from Andy Anderson of G. D. Searle. "As long as people are talking with one another, they'll stay motivated. The key to keeping people motivated is for them to understand what their goals are. Around here everyone knows that the goal is the budget. I believe the compensation plan is less important than this personal attention. People will work for a lot less money if they are given good supportive management."

Agreeing with the Hawthorne effect, Jerry McCloskey of Heinz U.S.A. notes that "motivation comes when the employees feel that the boss listens to their ideas and problems. A sales manager should proactively discuss with his or her people their present progress and future objectives. This is in addition to the formal semiannual review. Personal attention creates teamwork and a common bond, makes it possible to discuss negatives as well as positives openly and constructively, and clears up any misconception either party may have about the other person's worth."

MacDougal and Theory Y

Curtis MacDougal of MIT coined the term "Theory X" for the view held by many factory managers that human beings are essentially lazy, shirk responsibility, and will perform only those tasks they are specifically instructed to do. "Don't expect unless you inspect" is the motto of these managers.

MacDougal held that if people behaved that way, it was primarily because everyone expected them to behave that way. He espoused Theory Y, which held that if people are fully informed about the job and given an opportunity to seek better ways of doing it, they will show initiative and responsibility.

Tim Duncan of American Greetings feels that Theory X unfortunately does apply to some people, at least some of the time. "Some people," he says, "due to their past experiences or present situation, are just this way. They try to get along by doing the bare minimum. As a sales manager, it's your job to wake them up. There are several ways of doing this, and sometimes they only respect what you inspect. You owe them the chance to improve before taking further action.

"One rep that worked for me was this way. His home was in disrepair, the lawn was a foot tall, his car was messy, and I suspected that he and his wife weren't getting along. As he was only at 75 percent of his forecast, I made him a priority and worked with him weekly.

After a month of showing him that I cared for him professionally and personally, he began to respond. Today he is still with the company and performing at an above-average pace."

Maslow's Famous Pyramid

U.S. psychologist and philosopher Abraham Maslow postulated that all of us have a "hierarchy of needs" and are motivated by the lowest *unfilled* need. At the bottom of the pyramid are the physical needs: food, clothing, shelter, perhaps sex. Next comes security, the knowledge that these physical needs will continue to be met in the future. The third-level need is "belonging," to be accepted as a member of the family and a member of the group. Next step up the pyramid is the need for esteem, for self-respect, and the high regard of others. And finally, if all these needs are fulfilled, says Maslow, we strive for "self-fulfillment," the belief that we are using our natural abilities as best we can and leaving the world a better place for our passing through it.

Since we are motivated by the lower unfilled need, a starving man will strive for food but will not pursue higher needs such as recognition or a sense of belonging. But if the man has just had a square meal, he is not motivated by the offer of a pork chop; he now becomes motivated by the security needs and goes about ensuring that his next meal will be available.

One can observe this principle working in the sales force. Since most sales reps have fulfilled the three lower needs on the pyramid, the fourth need, usually expressed as "recognition," is a strong motivator for many of them.

"Recognition takes many forms," notes Jim Nichols of Dow Chemical. There are:

1. Recognition programs for one-time successes or events. The recognition should be made soon after the event and consist of public recognition (rep's name on a plaque or in the company magazine) plus a token tangible money gift.
2. Recognition programs that measure success over a period of time, such as a year. Examples are the million-dollar clubs often seen in real estate or insurance companies.
3. Awards for longevity, which tell others that the company appreciates loyalty.
4. Short notes from top management congratulating an employee on some achievement. This evidence that the company is aware and appreciative can have a long-term effect on the recipient.
5. "Focus dinners" with small groups of sellers to ask their opin-

ions about business decisions or the way the company conducts itself. People appreciate it when their opinions are valued.

"Constant recognition is a great motivator," agrees David A. Ruckman of Merrill Lynch. "Money is a great motivator in our business, but it's funny that often people who make the most money will exert more effort to win a souvenir coffee cup than to make a big commission. The rep making a million dollars is more motivated by winning a twenty-pound turkey in our Thanksgiving contest."

Adds Tim Duncan: "Maslow's theory is quite accurate, and we teach it to American Greetings managers. The theory is complicated as it applies differently at various times to each sales rep. Newer sales reps are usually motivated by physical needs, but as they become successful this changes. Another concept is that a rep can be motivated simultaneously by each level of the pyramid—the need for a bigger house (physical), job security, group acceptance, self-respect, and finally self-fulfillment. To apply this theory successfully, that manager must continually monitor the needs of each salesperson."

The concept of the lowest unfulfilled need comes into play when sales reps who have filled the three lower need levels learn that their company is about to be merged and that some sales jobs will be eliminated. Motivation quickly shifts to the second level: security.

Herzberg's Job Enrichment

Frederick Herzberg, while at the University of Pittsburgh, analyzed the motivation of a number of white-collar workers. He found that they were not inclined to exert a nickel's worth of extra effort by the existence of paid vacations, sick leaves, medical insurance, and the like. He called these the "hygienic factors"—they are taken for granted. If your company doesn't offer them, reps will transfer to a company that does, but the existence of these benefits does not stimulate extra effort.

What motivated workers, Herzberg found, was some influence over how a job was handled and the opportunity to develop their own abilities. Managers who applied this theory gave workers more freedom to make decisions, hence the term "job enrichment."

It would seem that salespeople have more freedom than most other workers in determining what strategies and tactics to use, but there is some evidence that sales productivity increases when sales reps are given more authority in making pricing decisions and handling complaints.

Skinner's Operant Conditioning

B. F. Skinner founded the "behavioristic" school of psychology, which holds that everything we do or believe has been "conditioned" into us throughout our lifetimes by rewards (positive reinforcement) for approved behavior and punishment of some kind (negative reinforcement) for disapproved behavior.

The application in job situations is to give workers immediate positive feedback by letting them know, as quickly as possible, when they have done something correctly or achieved some objective.

The obvious application to the sales force is to give prompt and frequent reports on sales results and to give reps some kind of positive reinforcement for any desired accomplishment. Or, as summarized by Stan Evans of Amway, "A big factor in motivation is recognizing performance and giving the rep a pat on the back."

"This system works," comments Tim Duncan, "if the positive feedback fills one of the Maslow needs, such as recognition or a feeling of belonging. I had a sales rep who constantly desired recognition. On every work-with he hinted or asked to be recognized, which I did. He even won the Sales Rep of the Year award. Later he was made my assistant, and I explained to him that in management 'pats on the back' are fewer. Doing your best at all times lets others recognize your efforts and gains their respect."

Howard Strelsin of Terminix International feels that the atmosphere in the branch office is the most important factor in motivation, and much of that atmosphere is the result of feedback. "Each branch has four or five sales reps," he explains. "They come in every morning no later than 8 A.M. and spend a few minutes 'calling the board.' There is a bulletin board showing the name of each rep, the mutually agreed-upon quota that the company has assigned to that rep, and also the quota each rep has set individually, usually higher than the company quota. They can see yesterday's figures on total sales and total dollars, offer suggestions to one another, discuss problems.

"It doesn't demotivate the person on the bottom; in fact, it spurs the rep to make a few extra calls that day to avoid showing a goose egg the next morning.

"After a brief group sales meeting, there is a ten-minute one-on-one daily check-in with each rep to discuss yesterday's results and today's game plan. There are also weekly personal development interview sessions in which manager and rep review general trends and activities and set specific goals for the upcoming week. The branch manager then makes a personal commitment as to the manager's follow-up activities and involvement with the rep in the field."

Managers often use ingenious methods of keeping their reps posted on sales results. For example, Bill Hammick of McKesson Drugs sends out weekly update letters showing results of every rep. "If anyone has a zero, he or she sees that zero on a report. Sales reps have an ego, they don't like to see that zero, they'll work hard to avoid it."

"One thing that helps us a lot," he adds, "is voice mail. I can dictate a message to all reps simultaneously, they hear it when they phone in, and this eliminates 'telephone tag.' If we're in the midst of a sales drive, I'll just read off the current results and add a few suggestions. All reps hear it when they phone in at 8 A.M., and they're off and running."

"Money, recognition, and advancement are the three most important motivators," says Robert Higham of CIBA. "Regarding achievement, if a rep wants to be promoted to district manager or to a home office position, the manager must react if the rep is qualified for advancement. The manager should discuss projects, objectives, or goals that the rep can accomplish to earn the promotion. Also, the manager should keep his or her immediate superior informed about this advancement program and about the completion of each project."

McClelland's Achievement Motive

David McClelland believed that most of us are motivated by the ability to set some kind of goal or task and achieve it. Meeting a sales quota gives one a feeling of "a job well done," even if no recognition or extra compensation is involved. We are motivated to attain our goals in order to enjoy that feeling of achievement. Tim Duncan feels that reps with a strong drive for achievement usually win promotions faster than those with other motivations.

On the subject of achievement, Jack Woods of United States Cellular adds: "It's important to ask them what their goals are and to help them reach their goals, not yours. You can't motivate people by holding up your goals—concentrate on theirs."

The Pygmalion Principle

Recent studies have indicated that some people behave in the way they are expected to behave. In an experiment, school teachers were told that two pupils, actually selected at random, would be star performers and that two others, also chosen at random, would have learning difficulties. Sure enough, those whom the teacher expected to be bright students *were* bright students, and those she expected to be dull turned out that way.

Does a sales rep perform the way the manager expects that rep to perform? Certainly the manager's expectation has a lot to do with it. In one study, a group of marginal insurance salesmen were placed with a manager who believed sincerely that their productivity could be increased. His group showed a greater percentage increase than similar groups of average salespeople whose managers expected average performance.

Tim Duncan reports that prospecting for new business is the part of his job he enjoys most and that he therefore expected his reps to do more prospecting. During his first month as manager of a new district, his team opened more new accounts than the total for the previous year.

Spur of Competition

Although the experts on motivation don't discuss it, many sales reps are highly motivated by a spirit of competition. They strive to win every contest even if they don't give a hoot about the prizes being offered. They get a charge out of taking business away from a competitor that is aside from any commissions they may earn.

"One means of motivating the local sales force," says Charles Williamson of Nabisco Foods Group, "is to split the group into two teams and let the losers serve the winners at a cookout. This increases team effort, which is a necessary ingredient of a good sales force."

Money and Motivation

Money is not mentioned as a motivator in any of these basic theories. That's because, except for a psychopathic miser, money is not an end in itself but only a means for attaining some other desired end. No matter what one's level of need on the Maslow pyramid—physical needs, security, esteem, self-actualization—money is a means of attaining it.

If a person does not desire any of the things money can buy, money is no motivator. We're all familiar with "plateaued" salespersons. They've paid off the mortgage, put their children through college, paid the initiation fees for all the proper clubs. They're not motivated by the possibility of earning additional money—the slight additional satisfaction it might bring them is not worth the extra effort required.

Tim Duncan disagrees. "I do believe money is a motivator for some sales representatives. I once had a rep who was truly money motivated. He judged his success by the amount of money he made. He kept giant growth charts behind his desk illustrating his progress toward his financial goals for the quarter and for the year."

Demotivation

Some sales managers feel that the problem is not so much to get salespeople motivated as it is to prevent them from being demotivated. The rep returns from a sales meeting all fired up, then hits five or six unsuccessful sales calls in a row. Under these circumstances it's hard to keep the motivational battery charged.

One answer to this problem is keeping score. If a sales rep introducing a new product finds that, on the average, ten calls will produce five orders, it's easier not to become discouraged by the five negatives. In fact, the sales rep is now motivated to try to increase the average from five out of ten to six or seven out of ten.

Common Motivators Versus Individual "Hot Buttons"

Some motivators seem to apply across-the-board to all members of the sales force, whereas others vary in importance with each individual. So sales managers are careful to provide as many of the common motivators as possible, at the same time determining what each individual wants out of life and helping him or her to attain it.

The common motivators—many of them noted earlier—are:

1. An effective sales compensation plan with extra rewards for extra accomplishments.
2. A manager who takes an interest in each individual—a form of recognition.
3. The feeling that he or she is doing an important job and that the manager, the company, and the community recognize that fact.
4. The feeling that "my company keeps me informed—there are no unpleasant surprises in store for me." It's demoralizing for a sales rep to find that a customer has learned something about the rep's company before the rep has. This may be related to Maslow's security need.
5. The knowledge that future income and retirement income are assured.

"Belief in the company's products or services is also important," adds Amway's Stan Evans. "Amway tries to have first-quality products, so you can always talk about how the products beat the competition. It motivates people to feel that they can offer to their friends and customers a better product and a better price than they're getting now. It makes them feel needed and useful, and not just sellers of something.

"The other thing that motivates a rep is knowing that he or she can do just as well as their sponsor who got them into the business. They can even surpass the sponsor if they wish. The rep says, 'Hey, I'm not going to be stuck in a rut or held back by a boss; I'm free to do my own thing.'

"The free-enterprise dream is to own your own business, and here's the opportunity to do that without risk and without a large investment, and you can do it part time. So with these advantages, why not give it all you have?"

Beyond such common denominators, the manager looks at each sales rep as an individual. Which is most important to him or her: money? security? advancement? recognition? self-development? And given the answer, how can the manager help the rep get more of what he or she wants by giving the company more of what it wants?

"Motivation is finding out what makes the individual tick," agrees Tom Dunning of Datacard Corp. "Some reps like money, some like prestige, some just like to be winners. And then feedback.

"If the rep likes money, talk about all the autos and boats and big houses the rep can enjoy. 'This deal will make you X dollars—isn't it worth working on?'

"With others, it's 'your name will be up in lights' or 'you'll be the most famous rep in the company.' Motivation is really like selling: Find out what they need and fill that need."

Tips on Motivation

The following participants offer tips on motivation.

Craig Hattabaugh, Aspen Technology:

It's important to control expectations. Just as the spin doctors of a political campaign work to put the desired slant on a news story, the manager must put the right spin on a person's expectations. The key to this is simply the truth. However, as simple as it sounds, I'll bet that 50 percent of all managers fail to do this. When pinned down by a subordinate on career path issues, it's easy to fall into the trap of promising things the manager can't deliver. Tell the truth, give people an accurate picture of where they stand, and clarify as best you can what they need to do to advance.

Bill Hammick, McKesson Drug Co.:

It's important to be consistent, not to try different gimmicks all the time.

Stan Evans, Amway:

One of the things we do more than anything else, in addition to good training, is to build self-confidence, getting them to believe that they're okay. People tend to doubt their own ability. Our biggest job is to make them believe in themselves.

Computer Sales Manager:

I, too, believe that motivation comes from within and that it is very necessary to hire hungry people. It is my opinion that hungry people can typically be identified by successes in their past jobs or in their academic or athletic experiences.

Frequent focus and accountability with positive reinforcement are keys to keeping people successful over a period of time. For example, if your business calls for making ten new presentations a week to be successful, then the manager should review that activity with the salesperson on a weekly basis and discuss it in detail.

Also, I believe that quotas should be broken down to the smallest increment possible, preferably weekly. If a salesperson is on a roll, he or she has to start producing again every week and not unintentionally relax because of one good week out of the month. Likewise, if a person starts off the month very slowly, a weekly quota system gives them a fresh new outlook each week. Using a weekly quota system also gives management a chance to recognize or reward individuals fifty-two times a year. Recognition and reward are, in my opinion, the highest possible motivators. Compensation is important, but over a long period of time it becomes less important to daily motivational needs and ego drive. Compensation within the sales organization is also an important motivator. Once again, ego drive enters the picture.

Proper goal setting with frequent reviews with the sales manager also helps an individual stay motivated. Consideration should be given not only to long-term and short-term career goals, but to personal goals as well. Discussions should even include things that relate to family, material possessions, physical well-being, and spiritual growth.

In summary, although motivation comes from within, it can certainly be enhanced by proper sales management. The sales manager should frequently discuss goals, activities, and productivity with each salesperson. Reps should be accountable in each of these sessions for what they are doing and how well they are achieving their goals. They should be praised frequently for progress and reprimanded for failure to take advantage of an opportunity to make progress. They should be listened to and counseled at every opportunity—weekly, if possible.

6

Field Coaching

If you wanted to improve your ability to play golf, or play the zither, or perform any other skilled task, which learning method would you find most effective?

- Reading a book on the subject
- Attending a seminar on the subject
- Actually playing golf (or a zither) with a pro observing you to reinforce what you do right and to correct what you do wrong

You probably selected number three. No book or lecture can be nearly as effective as on-the-job training under the eyes of a capable coach. In selling, on-the-job training takes place when the first-line manager makes routine calls with the seller to observe and coach.

Calls With a Noncoaching Objective

The word *routine*, as in "routine calls," is used advisedly. There are several totally different types of calls the manager makes with the sales rep. There's the "big deal" call, where the seller is right on the verge of landing a big contract and asks the manager to come along on the final call to lend weight to the presentation. Or there's the "fire-fighting" call, in which a big customer has a serious complaint and is about to go over to another supplier unless someone can mollify the customer quickly.

On both these calls, the one objective is to sell the deal or handle the complaint, regardless of whether the sales rep or the manager does most of the talking. Usually the manager does. And at the end of the call, the manager has not learned how the seller might have handled the situation alone; that was not the objective of the call.

Howard Strelsin of Terminix International says his company distinguishes among four different types of calls the manager makes with a rep:

1. The *demonstration* of a selling skill or a particular situation, usually made when training a new sales rep.
2. The *special situation* call, usually made with newer reps but sometimes with veterans, involving some situation the rep does not know how to cover.
3. The *sales blitz*, where the manager plans to spend a full day with a rep whose production is lagging. Manager and rep work as a team to sell as much business as possible, without any postcall critiques. This is a definite motivator.
4. The *evaluation* call, where the manager's objective is to observe the rep's performance without intervening. Getting the rep to review "what might have been done differently on the call" helps the rep gain insight into his or her deficiencies and overcome them.

A word about high-stakes calls: If a rep has an important call to make, the sales manager should always try to go with him or her. Not to take charge as far as making the presentation, but to give support.

The more a sales rep is exposed to the higher strategy of these important calls, the more valuable the experience. A good way to develop this experience is to include the rep in "business review" calls involving the company's key management and the customer's top people. The sales rep not only learns by observing, but becomes more important in the eyes of the customer.

"The rep need not be restricted to a mere sideline position on these important calls," says Tim Duncan of American Greetings. "In most situations of this nature, the manager knows what to expect on the call and can determine what roles he and the sales rep will take. If you plan for the call and prepare your material, you should be able to give a good amount of 'playing time' to your rep. The more time they get, the greater the learning experience and that is the key to their development."

The Observing/Coaching Call

A completely different type of call is the one the manager makes for the purpose of observing and coaching the seller. Here the manager's objective is not to sell but to observe. The manager doesn't interfere in the process, even if a sale is about to be lost. That's why observing and coaching can usually be done only on routine calls, not on the high-stake deal or fire-fighting calls.

Value of the Observing/Coaching Call

"Just like professional athletes, salespeople must regularly refresh their basic skills," says Rob McCoy of GTE. "These skills can be forgotten or 'taken for granted.' Coaching is the primary means of refreshing basic selling skills. And use a checklist!"

"Here at Searle," reports Andy Anderson, "the primary function for the district sales manager is to be with the representatives at least seventeen days per work month. We do provide an administrative day, if needed. Our sales operations group is consistently trying to cut out paperwork."

Alex Jones of Allstate Insurance Co. says: "Field coaching is a totally important part of the manager's job because, as the old saying goes, 'If it's worth doing right, it's worth doing it wrong at first while you're learning.' We learn from our mistakes. We're not going to be the masters of selling when we first begin that we will become five years later."

"If you go out and help them in the field," notes Bill Hammick of McKesson Drug Co., "see the things they're doing, see the problems they're having, that's a very important part of how they regard their manager.

"When I was out in the field, I sometimes had managers who never got out into the field. They'd send us letters telling us how to do something. We took their advice with large helpings of salt. When reps know you're out in the field a lot, they respect your opinions more."

Observing/Coaching Preparation

"What sort of advance notice should I give the sales rep that I plan to work with him or her?" a manager might ask. Some companies with a police-state mentality give no warning at all. The manager simply parks across the street from the sales rep's house early in the morning (a way of checking up on the rep's habitual starting time) and announces, "Surprise! I'm working with you today."

Most companies give the seller some advance notice. If the manager is interested in observing some particular type of call, such as new account calls, complaint calls, or new product introduction calls, the manager can ask the rep to arrange for some of the calls to be of that type.

"Usually a random sampling of sales calls is the most informative to the manager and beneficial to the salesperson," says the Communications Sales Manager. "With no time for advance preparation, the call can be a true observation of the rep's business-as-usual sales approach. This allows for a constructive review of the basic techniques: preparation, approach, positioning, proposing, overcoming objections, closing, and follow-up.

"Another excellent technique is 'cold calling' for one day. Select the individual and spend the day making customer satisfaction calls, product positioning calls, or closing calls all day. There is no truer method of refining sales skills than developing the art of cold calling."

"I try to give my reps lots of notice and ask to see a variety of selling situations," says Alina Bilodeau of The Clorox Company. "This allows for adequate preparation and planning. With new sales representatives, this notice defines the expectations and provides a sense of trust and security between sales manager and sales representative. In the later development of a sales rep's career, 'surprise' work-withs test the rep's consistency of presentation as well as performance under pressure. In general, the surprise work-withs are limited in number and skewed toward those whose performance is suspect."

"Giving sales reps time to prepare for the work-with will allow them to get much more out of the time spent together," notes Tim Duncan of American Greetings. "They can accumulate their questions and take you to accounts where they have been less than successful. I always send a letter two weeks in advance telling them the dates I'll be with them and what I need to cover with them. I also emphasize that this is 'their time,' that I am there to assist them, so let's use the time in the way that will be most beneficial to them.

"You must also be careful not to be totally led by the rep. Do your homework, analyze the rep's reports, and be aware of the accounts where there is potential trouble. On the first day ask if the problem account is in the day's schedule; if not ask the rep to call on them the second or third day.

"If you give no advance notice of your work-with, you will make those days less productive. First, the rep will become defensive, thinking 'What am I doing wrong? What is he or she trying to catch me at?' The work-with will be negative rather than positive.

"When I began at American Greetings, my district manager would phone me at 7 A.M. and tell me to meet him at 8:30 A.M. My mind immediately began to race with 'what's wrong?' and I didn't get much out of the day. Eventually I realized that this was his style and I learned to live with it, but I still think advance preparation makes the work-with more productive."

Tips on Observing/Coaching

How often should a manager work with each individual sales rep? As often as possible, which will rarely be too often in view of all the other demands on the manager's time. Two days per quarter with each rep is a goal some corporations set.

Tim Duncan, American Greetings:

I plan for six "regular call" work-withs per year, each one a two-day or if necessary three-day session. That's the goal, but it's not always possible so it's important to keep logs on whom you've worked with and who's due for attention.

Jerry McCloskey, Heinz U.S.A.:

Heinz U.S.A. requires that each middle-management supervisor spend a minimum of two days a month working with each sales rep. The supervisor usually has three or four reps to manage. The district manager is required to work a minimum of one-third day per rep per month on the average.

Bill Hammick, McKesson Drug Co.:

With fifteen sales reps reporting to me, I spend five or six of the twenty working days per month in the field. The length with each rep varies, two or three full days with a new rep, just one quick call on an important customer with an established rep. I don't follow a rigid pattern such as being with each rep three times a year. I see the reps when they need help. If I'm not out in the field one hundred days a year, I don't feel that I'm doing my job.

Jim Nichols, Dow Chemical USA:

Field coaching can be supplemented by coaching accomplished through a review of written communications and call reports. These are not a substitute for traveling with a field seller, but it can complement that activity to enable the manager to do as much coaching as possible with all reps. For example, a new seller should write call reports on all calls made during the first three to six months. This enables the manager to observe from a distance what the seller is doing and spot the need for coaching much earlier. Call reports are also an important field coaching tool for experienced sellers at more complex accounts. The manager can apply the same techniques, although less frequently than with the new seller.

Coaching the Star Rep

Some managers ask, "How can I coach so-and-so?—his or her selling skills are better than mine." One answer: What was the name of Paderewski's piano teacher? Nobody knows, but that somebody helped Paderewski improve his techniques without being able to duplicate them.

Don House of NCR observes that Jack Nicklaus won a Master's title after a putting tip from his son, who will never be as great a golfer as his father.

No seller operates at 100 percent of his or her abilities. Remember the story of the farmer who asked the Department of Agriculture to stop sending him bulletins because "I ain't farming now half as well as I know how to do it." Everyone improves by being coached.

"So-and-so is my star salesperson. She doesn't need any coaching; my time is better spent with the sellers who aren't so hot." Managers should never neglect the star. For one thing, they'll pick up ideas they can pass along to the other sales reps. Moreover, having the boss spend a few days in the field with the rep is a form of recognition. One way to demotivate a salesperson is to ignore him or her.

"You can't totally neglect the ones who don't need help," agrees Bill Hammick of McKesson Drug Co. "They still need the stroking. They may pretend they don't care about numbers, but when you sit down with them and tell them what a good job they're doing, they'll walk away a couple of feet taller."

"I think all managers are somewhat guilty of ignoring their best performers because they're striving to develop the not-so-successful individuals," says Tim Duncan. "We must also work with the more successful because neglect will demotivate them. This is a good opportunity to accentuate the positive and let these people know that you appreciate the good job they're doing.

"When I was first assigned a new district, I analyzed the reps' reports to find out where each really stood. My first inclination was to work hard with those individuals performing below par. After three months I noted that, of the fourteen reps, I had worked with the six lowest performers two or more times each, with the three middle ones once each, and never with the top five.

"My next move was to work with everyone at least once, and I found that the top five had weaknesses too. The work-withs gave me an opportunity to develop them and to provide some positive reinforcement.

"No matter how successful the sales rep is, there is always some aspect of the rep's performance that can be improved. I had a sales rep who was extremely smooth, confident, knowledgeable of the product, a good listener, who closed a high percentage of calls.

"He told me that he was working harder than ever, but his rate of success was not increasing. I worked with him at his request and as the day progressed one thing became clear. He used the same sales technique with everyone, regardless of their position. He didn't alter his approach to fit the customer. Instead of seeing them as individuals with different needs and priorities, he viewed them all the same way. He was playing a hit-or-miss game that succeeded only in those situations that happened to fit his standard style.

"We worked on the 'leaf, tree, and forest' concept that each individual in a retail chain has a different role to play. To increase your chance of success, you must determine what's important to the specific customer and present your program in a light that will satisfy the needs of both the individual and the chain."

"Working with a star can be a learning experience for the manager," says Alina Bilodeau of The Clorox Company. "I feel we should always be open to new selling ideas, as well as being able to pick up ideas from the star that we can pass along to a struggling salesperson.

One plus one equals four. Two consecutive days spent with the seller are more valuable to the manager than two single days a month or two apart. If the manager is going to be there for only one day, the rep can fairly easily arrange for the manager to see only the type of customer the rep wants the manager to see. All the calls can be lovey-dovey customers or hard-nosed negotiators.

But if the manager is still there the second day, the sales rep runs out of screened customers in that part of the territory. The manager is more likely to see a representative cross section of customers. Besides, the evening between the two days is an opportunity to have a relaxed dinner conversation with the seller and perhaps with the spouse.

Making Field Coaching Work

Should the manager hold a critique after each call or observe two or three calls to see if there is a pattern? Should the manager correct a mistake the first time it is observed, or wait to see if it is repeated?

"The manager should comment on any undesirable behavior as soon as possible," advises Andy Anderson of G. D. Searle. "Even if it isn't important, it will grow to be important. I would rather have a manager say to a rep: 'You know, on this situation if you had done thus-and-so you would have been more effective.' That's far less confrontational than to say, 'Mr. Rep, I've seen you do thus-and-so on the last four calls.'

"If the manager observes a number of things that need correction, he should pick the two or three most important. If there are radical problems, it's best to say, 'Let's run back to the hotel; I think there are a lot of things we didn't cover' and try to place the blame somewhere else to keep a harmonious relationship between the manager and the rep."

Before effective field coaching can take place, there must be agreement between manager and seller as to the "yardstick" for a good call. This may have been established in the sales rep's initial training or in district meetings.

"There must be a clearly defined, instructed, coached, and disciplined sales approach for the company," insists Rob McCoy of GTE. "This will specify the fundamentals for selling the company's products and will vary depending upon the complexity of the products, the marketing characteristics, and the sales cycle. The process may vary dramatically from a single-call transaction driven by price to an eighteen-month to two-year sales cycle driven by sophisticated technological considerations. At either end of the spectrum, the sales process must be thoroughly understood before constructive field coaching can take place."

"We call this the up-to-standard," comments Tim Duncan. "There is a basic criteria of the essential elements needed for a good call. I challenge my people to go one step farther and get the most they can out of each call."

It's desirable for the manager to have a few relaxed minutes with the seller—perhaps over breakfast—to give the seller a chance to ask any questions, make any explanations, in general clear the air.

Before each call, there are two preliminary steps.

1. The manager and the rep review the status of the account and the objectives of the call.

Rob McCoy of GTE says about work-with: "Knowledge of the client is vital to sales success. Therefore precall evaluation should include a review of the customer, the history of the account, and the current situation."

Tim Duncan of American Greetings adds, "Before the call, I take time to review the situation and our objectives, discuss what we expect the customer's reactions to be, establish our negotiating position, and create a few different approaches to allow flexibility."

Jim Nichols of Dow Chemical says, "Part of coaching is an advance discussion of the seller's plan for his or her accounts in general, so that both the manager and the seller have a broad perspective as to what is to be accomplished at each account throughout the year. Before each call, the manager and the seller—and anyone else involved in the call—should have a thorough discussion of the objective of the call. This leads to better communication and also stresses to the seller that he or she shouldn't be making the call unless there is a specific objective for it."

2. The manager and sales rep must agree on the roles each is to play. If the manager wants to shut up and just observe, that should be clear to the sales rep. Or perhaps the sales rep will handle most of the call, handing the ball to the manager to introduce a new product. They may agree on some secret signals the rep can use when he or she wants the manager to chime into the conversation, or that the manager can use when he or she wants the rep to toss the ball to the manager.

"Before each call," advises Howard Strelsin of Terminix, "the manager should let the sales rep know what part each of them is to play in the call. The manager may play devil's advocate, being on the customer's side, so the customer won't feel that two salespeople are ganging up on him.

"I've asked questions of the salesperson just to make sure certain points were put across for the customer. This is not intervening, because I don't give the answers. It's asking questions on behalf of the customer. If the rep is floundering, I may say, 'Joe, why don't you tell them about such-and-such.' This makes sure the point will be covered without making it appear that the salesperson was negligent. We try to get the sales reps to recognize their own weaknesses and then to improve them by role-playing."

"Obviously in the initial phases of training you may want to set examples for the rep," says Alex Jones of Allstate Insurance. "But on later calls, it's important to have a clear understanding, before you make the call, of who's going to make the presentation. If you want the rep to make the presentation, let the rep do it, mistakes and all. You get involved only if the rep asks you to in the midst of the presentation. Just listen carefully and reserve all your remarks until later."

"On joint calls with a big customer," says Bill Hammick of Mc-Kesson, "I tell the sales rep before we go in, 'You're carrying the ball. You're making the presentation. If I see you're having trouble with one of the customer's questions, I'll step in.' This occurs only when the customer asks some unusual question that only management can answer. But if the call follows the usual pattern, I'll stay in the background.

"I've seen some managers who never say a word, ever. They let the rep sink or swim, regardless. Those managers will tell you they'll do the coaching after the call, but sometimes the rep likes to see the manager handle problems right there in front of them."

"I tell my salespeople, before calling with them, that 'I won't let you fall but I will let you stumble,' meaning that if they're going to make mistakes it's better for them to do it when I'm there so I can provide feedback," says Dave Singer of Cellular One. "There should be a clear procedure by which the sales rep can be the primary person responsible for the call but can involve the manager when necessary."

The most difficult task for the manager, on the observing type of call, is to keep the mouth shut and fingers out of the machinery. It's not uncommon for a seller to say, "When the boss travels with me, I just relax—the manager does all the talking." This type of manager totally fails to achieve the objective of the call, which was to observe the rep in action.

"This is true," confesses Tim Duncan. "After being promoted into management, I worked with a rep on a prospect call for a college bookstore. We planned the call and went in. I sat on a sofa in the rear of the room and my rep sat next to the store manager. Everything went well and as the call developed I really began biting my tongue. But before I knew what happened, I found myself leaning over the store manager's desk, pointing to the store blueprints, and really taking charge. When I realized what had happened, I stood straight up, led the conversation back to the rep, walked back to my seat, sat down, and shut up. Old habits die hard."

Tips on Fading Into the Wallpaper

♦ Have the sales rep "downplay" or "low key" the introduction. Instead of "This is my district manager, Tom Jones," the rep might say, "This is Tom Jones" or "This is Tom Jones; he's making a few calls with me this week." The buyer may respond to the rep, "Fine! By the way, where have you been for the last six months?" That, or something similar, means the buyer knows exactly what's going on and is willing to play the game.

♦ Take the back row seat. In most people's offices, there is a chair right next to the desk for the key visitor and one or two in more out-of-the-way places. The rep sits in the hot seat; the manager stays in the background.

♦ Keep quiet! Bite your tongue! It's almost impossible to do, but the manager should resolve to come as close to it as possible.

♦ "Establish signals for the call." This comes from Tim Duncan of American Greetings. "When the rep gets into trouble, have him tug on his ear or give some other signal. That way the manager can remain a total observer until the rep asks for help."

♦ If the buyer directs a question at you, bounce it back to the rep. "Yes, that's an important question. Mary was mentioning that as we were driving here. Mary, tell him about . . ."

Tim Duncan adds, "As you bounce the question back to the rep, requalify the rep as being experienced in this area: 'Mary had a situation very similar to that. How did you handle it, Mary?' "

♦ Dave Singer of Cellular One suggests, "If the customer pays too much attention to you, the manager, make solid eye contact with the customer and guide that eye contact over to the sales rep."

♦ Don't interfere unless the seller is making some kind of misrepresentation that might get you in legal trouble if you ignore it. Don't jump in to save the sale—otherwise how will you ever find out whether the sales rep would have tried to close? If you do rescue the rep, instead of heeding your advice during the postcall critique, the seller will be thinking, "I would have done that if you hadn't interfered."

Tips on the After-Call Conference

Regarding the curbstone conference or critique session after the call, should the manager hold a critique after each call, or observe two or three calls to see if there is a pattern? Should the manager point out each mistake immediately after the call or wait to see if it recurs?

♦ "You hold the discussion after each call," says Alex Jones of Allstate, "because it's important that the person learn from whatever mistakes might have been made on the call so they won't be repeated on the next call. By the same token, if the rep does an excellent job in some areas, by complimenting him or her on it you build the rep's confidence."

♦ Ask the sales rep to critique the call first. One of the most important habits you can inculcate in reps is to mentally review the strengths and weaknesses of each call immediately afterward.

♦ Reinforce what the sales rep did well. This is more than a mere pat on the back to make the upcoming criticism more palatable; it helps to engrain the good habits.

• Don't cover too much ground. You may have ten or twelve suggestions you'd like to make, but what seller can keep ten or twelve things in mind on the next call? Most of us can't even remember the Ten Commandments. So make two or three important points about this call, and let the rest go for another time.

• Use questions to get the sales rep to see the weaknesses—even if they have to be leading questions.

• Try to get the sales rep to suggest the better ways. When you give advice, it may suffer to some extent from the NIH ("not invented here") syndrome. But if the rep thinks of it, he or she will be more likely to believe in it and actually apply it at the next opportunity.

• Most difficult of all: try to get some kind of feedback from the sales rep. What you think you said and what the rep thinks you said may be shockingly different. So end each critique session by asking, "Let's wrap it up. What would you say were the most important points we developed in this conversation?"

• "What you are trying to do is get the sales rep into the habit of analyzing what he or she is doing," says Tom Dunning of Datacard Corp. "The fact that the rep makes a mistake is not important; what's important is that the rep recognizes the mistake and deals with it.

"Coaching should be as impersonal as possible. You don't want to criticize the person, you want to criticize the action. It's a tough distinction, but sales is an ego game and you need to keep the reps pumped up or they're not going to do the things you want them to do. Start with what was done right on the call, keep it positive, then go into what might have been done differently.

"This same kind of postcall analysis should be done after a demonstration call made by the manager. Anybody can make a mistake."

• "The most critical part of the critique is to leave this sales rep on a positive note," comments Jerry McCloskey of Heinz U.S.A. "Always end the session by reinforcing the good attributes and showing your faith in the rep's skills.

"My personal method of follow-up is to communicate the next steps via a memo or letter. I encourage the rep and I thank the rep for the rewarding day, then hit home on goals and focus on the details that need attention.

"And while talking about the call and the critique, let's not forget that the true measure of a good salesperson is in what happens after the call—in other words, the follow-up. The best salespeople keep their accounts confident that nothing will be left to chance. If there is a request for documentation, it will be handled immediately. If some action is requested on a customer complaint, it is handled immediately. The follow-up can make or break the sale."

7

Reports and Communications

Paperwork! Call reports! Expense accounts! Forms, forms, forms!

Every salesperson hates paperwork. All salespeople complain about it with equal vehemence, whether they have to submit three reports a week or thirty.

Yet the manager needs those reports, accurate and on time. How do we harmonize the company's need for the information with the sales rep's reluctance to supply it?

From Don House of NCR comes succinct advice most managers will agree with: "Keep reports in both directions to a minimum and make them as concise as possible. There's no sense in unnecessary verbiage. Write only what is necessary, and that in the most precise and clear form possible."

"Communication is essential to any sales force," comments Tim Duncan of American Greetings. "The manager cannot manage unless he or she knows 'what's going on out there.' Communication is, of course, a two-way street, with both manager and rep taking responsibility for it.

"If reps aren't providing sufficient or accurate information, it's up to the manager to get it from them. Moreover, reps derive value from the fact that their managers care about what and how they are doing."

Automation has eliminated many of the reports formerly typed or handwritten. "Automation of the sales force is very important and very difficult to measure," says Rob McCoy of GTE, "but the payoff is often *big* in terms of efficiency, morale, and price. Frito Lay and Federal Express have automated their route sales and have achieved tremendous success in all three areas. If you don't think so, just ask one of their route salespeople—but allow plenty of time for the answer!"

We first look at reports originating with the sales rep and then at reports the rep receives from the company or manager.

Call/Expense Reports From Reps

"Call reports and expense reports should be required at the same frequency, ideally every week," says Tim Duncan. "An expense report should not be accepted without the accompanying call report.

"We ask our reps and managers to fill out their call reports as soon as they return to their car after the call. That enables them to analyze the results while the call is still fresh in their minds. On Friday they simply fine-tune their reports, add that day's expense, and drop it in the mail.

"American Greetings recently added voice mail for the sales force. I can't say enough about how great this is. Information that doesn't require a paper trail can be communicated instantly. Customer service has greatly improved—a manager can get information to or from a rep and respond to a customer's question within an hour or two. Even aside from the customer service aspect, voice mail is a great tool for managers. Instead of spending an evening on the phone getting a message to the sale reps, the manager can record it once and send it simultaneously to all reps.

"When a manager works with a rep, the manager fills out a manager's call report. In addition to standard information such as the name of the rep and dates worked with, the form includes information on forecast attainment, credit percentage, late call percentage, and merchandiser work. The rest of the form summarizes the day's activities in terms of accounts called on, length of calls, and important occurrences. Across the bottom of the manager's report is a section noting how well the rep performed during that work-with period. The format is the same as that of the rep's annual evaluation. This information not only guides the manager in coaching the rep, but ensures that reps will never be surprised during an annual evaluation, since they have been receiving feedback right along."

Paperwork Audits

Paperwork has a way of growing like a cancer, especially in large companies. At least every two years, a manager should take a fresh look at every item of paperwork to see how it might be simplified. If this is the responsibility of someone back at headquarters, the manager can at least offer suggestions.

The three questions to ask about each report are:

1. Do we really need this information, or can this report be eliminated completely? "Question the usefulness of every piece of paper," advises Dave Singer of Cellular One.
2. If we do need it, can it easily be combined with some other report so that two pieces of paper do the work of one?
3. How can the report be simplified?

"Keep written reports to you at a minimum and as cogent as possible. But if they're required, they're required," says Tom Dunning of Datacard Corp. "You can't cut any slack on the necessary ones. For example, reps who don't do their expense reports on time are just sloppy businesspersons. They just 'gotta' do them."

"It's important that the manager know, at least on a weekly basis, what's going on in the field," says Alex Jones of Allstate, "because it sometimes takes a minimum of thirty days to turn things around. If you don't get reports at least weekly, and if one of your agents has a week or two of real bad results, by the time you start working with the agent thirty days have elapsed and it may take another thirty to get the agent back to par."

"Sell" the Sales Force on Paperwork's Value

Salespeople especially resent paperwork when they feel that it is merely being filed and forgotten. If the information it contains is really being used in analyzing, planning, or controlling, let the sales force know, at sales meetings or in newsletters, how it is being used.

"If you can't sell the sales force on the value of the information to them, linking it to increased sales, improved customer satisfaction, or larger profits, it is very likely that the information doesn't have enough value to warrant collecting it," comments Robert McCoy of GTE.

Show Sellers How to Use the Information

The information in sales reports can usually be very valuable to the sales rep in determining how to invest scarce selling time for the maximum payoff.

For each type and size of customer, the seller can determine ratios like the average order size per call, the number of calls per order, and the relationship between call frequency and resulting sales. This enables the seller to get the greatest return per hour of selling time.

"One of the oldest and most discussed subjects with first-line managers," says Charles Williamson of Nabisco Foods Group, "is getting sales reps to keep sufficient records so that they know, on a daily or weekly basis, their standings toward that month's forecast or sales goal.

"Most managers rely on sending out sales standings on a weekly basis. We have had much success with requiring the sales rep to keep a daily record of total sales, as well as sales of certain products or product groups. This information is then sent to my attention every Friday. This keeps sales reps fully informed at all times, and as a result more forecasts are reached and more incentives are won."

Help Develop Efficient Work Habits

Efficient methods of tackling each type of paperwork can minimize the total time it consumes.

For example, call reports, unless they are very complicated, take less time if they are filled out immediately after each call, rather than waiting until the evening and then trying to recall details of the first calls that morning. However, complicated reports or correspondence that require reference books or calculations take less total time if the sales rep lets them accumulate and then handles several of them at the same time, rather than doing each one individually.

"Organizational skills are critical to the new sales rep to avoid being swamped with paperwork," comments Alina Bilodeau of Clorox. "I find myself asking probing questions to see if paperwork is being handled efficiently. I even go so far as to visit the sales rep's home or office to see if their filing system presents any problems."

Reports From Company or Manager

"Reports from the company or region are important in getting sales reps to realize that they're part of a team," notes Howard Strelsin of Terminix International. "They see how their individual goals fit in with branch goals, regional goals, divisional goals, company goals.

"Competitive sales reps want to know how they stand relative to other sales reps. They get a 'sales ladder' report from their region each month showing how each branch did, how each rep did, how the service people did, a whole page of closing percentages. Sample: John Jones got fifty leads, closed twenty-five of them, a 50 percent closing average. He had a total of sixty-five sales, so forty were creative, not based on leads."

"As for communication from the first-line manager to the field," says Tom Dunning of Datacard Corp., "I'd rather do that in person, but some written communication is necessary. They get such a flurry of paperwork that I hate to add to it."

"It's extremely important to put out recognition bulletins," advised Alex Jones of Allstate Insurance. "I put out a Top Five recognition letter but don't list the results of those on the bottom. That's motivation by fear and I don't think it works. I try to dwell on the positive and recognize the people who are doing the good jobs. The ones at the bottom know who they are, and the others know who they are, so there's no use putting out a bulletin with a zero opposite their names."

Reports Andy Anderson of G.D. Searle: "I ask the regional sales directors to publish a monthly regional bulletin. The district sales managers also will put out a monthly correspondence as it relates to their specific district to ensure they have their own identity. Every one of our ninety-eight districts has a specific name for its own identity, e.g., Metro District, Rocky Mountain District, Lombardi District.

"I caution field managers about writing too many letters to their representatives because it's like yelling at young children: you can send so much information that the receiver becomes deaf. I recommend handwritten messages on reports rather than a letter with the report attached. We have very little written correspondence between rep and manager because 'I'm busy with paperwork' is always an excuse for not making calls."

Jerry McCloskey of Heinz U.S.A. agrees. "Communication done properly can be a real support, but overzealous managers can kill the golden goose with too much data. A good manager will think twice about what must really be in the hands of the field. I knew two managers who were so enmeshed in reports that their field reps felt insecure about them."

"In communicating with reps," advises Bill Hammick of McKesson Drug, "try to be as consistent as possible, not up one day and down the next. Even if a rep goofs, be consistent in how you handle the goofs—don't ignore one and then land on the rep for the next.

"Getting reports in on time is not a problem but 'communication' is a whole different problem.

"How do reps relate to the customer service people in the office? Some field sales reps make the mistake of approaching the inside service people in a negative way: 'You people screwed up again.' Others are wise enough to take the friendly approach: 'I need your help again.' "

8
Local Sales Meetings

The first-line manager's responsibility for his or her own local meetings can vary anywhere from an informal fifteen-minute session every Monday morning for a city sales staff to a three-day quarterly or semiannual meeting at a resort location for a widely scattered sales force.

If carefully planned and intelligently (not necessarily expensively) staged, these local meetings can provide valuable information, training, and motivation. If poorly handled, they can be boring and can actually discourage and demotivate the sales force.

If the meeting is to be held outside the office, the manager picks a suitable location. This is one area in which you travel first class—not deluxe, perhaps, but certainly first class. A sales meeting is an important event to even the most blasé sales rep, so the surroundings must be attractive and pleasant.

This chapter covers the basic groundwork, step-by-step suggestions for planning sales meetings, descriptions of specific meetings of specific companies, and checking out the site.

The Basic Groundwork

Following are contributors' suggestions on how to hold sales meetings.

D. M. House, NCR:

Don't hold unnecessary meetings. We get instructions from management to hold a meeting on some subject that may not relate to this district. Never hold a meeting just so you can fill out a form and report that you held the meeting. It's the first-line manager's duty to go to management and convince them that it would be a waste of time. We've done this for years and it works very well.

But if there are subjects that are pertinent to the current field efforts, it's the manager's job to recognize situations that require meetings so his or her people can be successful with some new product or program that's coming down the pike.

Rob McCoy, GTE:

Sales meetings can be classified into three types:

1. Weekly administration and review
2. Quarterly or monthly reviews
3. Sales rallies

The weekly meetings provide a brief opportunity to review key sales programs, product or pricing changes, promotions, and individual sales achievements. They also provide a needed opportunity to review administrative requirements. This is often best achieved by having a breakfast meeting.

The quarterly or monthly reviews provide the opportunity for the team to review its progress toward objectives and at times to develop improvements. This meeting also allows time for major production/promotion announcements and is a vital opportunity for presenting recognition and other rewards. It should be a celebration of successes.

The sales rally should be reserved for very major events, such as an annual kickoff or the launching of a major product or promotion. It is crucial that these meetings focus only on positive aspects, because their purpose is to inform *and motivate*, mostly the latter.

Charles Williamson, Nabisco Foods Group:

Paperwork may be tops on sales reps' "most unwanted" list, but unnecessary sales meetings rank a close second. In my thirty-six years I have attended and conducted many sales meetings. I'm sorry to report that many I attended and many I conducted were not works of art.

However, it is possible to run a successful sales meeting—where the sales force leaves wanting to go straight to the territory to begin using all the ideas that were generated. In almost every instance, this type of simulation was generated by using the group method of mixing it up and going "out of the box," which means researching unrelated companies or products to see how they do.

The final plan of action was one to which each team member had contributed some input. Getting everyone involved is the key to a successful sales strategy meeting. And speaking of strategy meetings, keep mundane information and criticism out of them!

Alex Jones, Allstate Insurance:

It's important to have meetings on a regular basis, whether daily, weekly, monthly, or quarterly. I know that some straight life insurance sales managers have meetings almost every morning, but if you have busy people who are producing well, they don't have time for an overabundance of meetings.

The important things to remember are: (1) notify the reps well ahead of time so they can plan their schedules, (2) let the reps know what's going to be covered in the meeting so they can make any preparations or bring any materials (or questions!), (3) conduct the meeting in a comfortable environment in a room of adequate size in which the participants are neither refrigerated nor overheated, (4) start the meeting on time, and (5) make the content of the meeting interesting and educational. There's no bigger waste of time than to go to a two- or three-hour meeting and find that the material is redundant, irrelevant, and totally uninteresting.

Sales skill development is more of a field job, but some skill development can be done in meetings. Role playing is effective. Also, there's as much learned by agents hearing other agents' ideas as there is by listening to the manager. Managers with multiple lines who aren't out in the field all the time get rusty. Maybe there are newer and better ways of doing things, so why not exchange ideas among the agents who are doing the job?

Stan Evans, Amway:

Try to get as many of your people as possible involved in the meeting. Pick out certain ones who are doing outstanding jobs and in advance of the meeting, assign them a topic to cover. This does two things: it gives them recognition and it provides good training for the entire group. It's the manager's job to say, "Okay, here's what this one is doing really well. I'll have him cover that topic." Suppose that's the appointment. Somebody else does an excellent close, so you have the first one talk about the appointment and the second talk about the close, and between the two you have an excellent presentation. The manager needn't do all the talking. It's the manager's job to line up the presenters and time the program correctly.

Dave Singer, Cellular One:

Local meetings can be a valuable tool if used correctly, but too often they are conducted because they are expected, or because that's the way the former manager did it. There must be a purpose for every sales meeting.

Jack Woods, United States Cellular:

View local meetings as an open forum in which ideas can be exchanged. Avoid being dictatorial in the way you conduct the meeting; get everyone to participate.

Craig Hattabaugh, Aspen Technology:

Schedule around recreational activity. It goes against many managers' grain to "waste" time on golf (for example), but that chance to meet informally, one-on-one with speakers, sales managers, and other reps is where some of the best transfers of information happens.

Planning the Meeting

The first step in planning a sales meeting is essential but difficult, because it requires a lot of head scratching. The step is to set clear-cut objectives as to what you intend to accomplish with the meeting.

The key question is: "What do I want the sales force to *do* as a result of this meeting that they might not do if they hadn't attended it?"

The meeting will usually have several objectives (not too many!), but each of them should be specific and, if humanly possible, measurable—not just "Sell more of Product X," but "Each salesperson should sell 15 percent more of Product X." Not just "Route themselves better," but "Make 10 percent more sales calls with a 15 percent decrease in mileage driven."

The next step is a bit easier. Ask yourself: "In order to accomplish each of these objectives, what will each sales rep have to *know*, what will he or she have to *do*, and what will each of them have to *believe*?"

Answers to these questions give you the contents of three different kinds of meeting activities:

1. What do they need to know? Your answer to this question defines the knowledge or information portion of your meeting.

2. What do they need to do? This is either skill training or proce-
   dural information.
3. What do they need to believe? This is the motivational or
   inspirational part of the meeting.

Meeting Themes

You may want to build the entire meeting around a dramatic theme. The
theme is repeated in the announcements of the meeting, banners at the
meeting site, title on program, mastheads on any handouts, and taglines
of speeches.

Themes can be derived from such things as:

- Sporting events: win the Indy 500, the Superbowl, the World
  Series, Kentucky Derby, Triple Crown.
- Athletics: let's hit par, make a touchdown, make a home run,
  break the tape, fast start, jump the hurdles, scale the mountain.
- Gambling: hit the jackpot, fill the flush, hold all the aces.
- Learning: earn your PhD (the initials standing for some activity
  of your company), join the Whiz Kids.
- Any currently popular television program.
- A current news event such as a presidential election.

Meeting Content

There are two important fundamentals for meeting content:

1. Allow plenty of time for audience participation. The smaller
groups involved in the meetings of first-line managers make this
possible. In addition to unrushed question-and-answer periods, plan
participative sessions such as idea exchanges, experience exchanges,
problem-solving sessions, and so on.

2. Don't try to cover too much ground. Figure that every speaker,
every Q&A period, every activity will take longer than your first esti-
mate. Allow a half-hour cushion in each morning and afternoon schedule. When a meeting planner tries to cram too much into the allotted
time, the first thing eliminated is audience participation—and the sales
force returns home frustrated rather than fulfilled.

"Review all speakers' material," advises Craig Hattabaugh. "If you
allow them thirty minutes, they'll bring enough material for two hours.
Caution them in advance if they're trying to cover too much ground and
be strict about finishing times."

Information Portions

Follow these rules concerning the meeting information portion:

1. Make a careful outline of the information to be presented and have it visible to participants in the form of a flipchart that stays in view, or an outline in their handout material.
2. Use visuals as much as possible. Overhead transparencies are better than slides, as they can be used in a lighted room, enable the speaker to maintain eye contact with the audience, and are less conducive to napping.
3. If the nature of the material permits it, use demonstrations or application exercises in which the audience can participate.
4. Allow plenty of time for questions during (if feasible) and after the presentation.
5. Get some form of feedback to make sure participants have understood the material.

Skill Development Portions

The best way to develop a skill during a meeting is to let participants practice that skill under simulated conditions. Many skills can be practiced in this way. If you want to develop reps' skills in planning sales calls, give them a planning form and several hypothetical situations and let them, individually or in teams, plan the calls. If you want to develop skills in routing themselves more effectively, give them a map of a hypothetical territory and see who can develop the best routing.

The most obvious skill practice, however, is role-playing. Many salespeople fear and resent any kind of role-playing or practice sales calls, at sales meetings. And in many cases, rightly so. The very worst the sales manager can do is to call upon some sales rep, on the spur of the moment, to walk up to the front of the room and demonstrate a sales call for the audience. Reps who are totally self-possessed in front of the toughest purchasing agent may develop such stage fright in front of their peers that they shake like an aspen leaf when trying to handle their price lists.

Role-playing can be an effective, nonthreatening learning experience if these guidelines are followed:

1. Make it clear why you are doing the role-playing. The purpose is not to test the individual, but to create a hypothetical sales call, like a laboratory specimen, which the audience can then analyze to develop multiple ways of handling various sales situations.

2. Instead of asking one or two sales reps to role-play calls in front of the entire group, let everyone make practice calls in small groups.

3. Give each sales rep plenty of time to prepare the call, even to make notes and refer to them during the call.

4. Be sure to control the person who takes the part of the buyer. For some reason, sales reps given this opportunity seem to take delight in digging up every objection they have heard in their lifetimes. The "sales rep" never gets a chance to finish a sentence. The manager can be the buyer if possible. When others take that part, the manager warns them: "You may never have seen a polite purchasing agent in your life, but you're going to be one now. Listen politely. Ask questions if you wish, but don't bring up more than two or three objections during the entire call. If, and only if, the seller tries to close, you may buy or not buy, depending upon what you think a real buyer might do in the circumstances."

5. Let the person who has done the selling be the first to critique his or her performance. If there has been some obvious deficiency in the practice call, it's more face-saving for the seller to point it out rather than to have others remind him or her of it.

6. Start the general critique of the sales call by asking all the observers to comment upon what was done well in the call. Then ask for suggestions as to what might have been done differently.

To give everyone a chance to practice a sales call, use the round robin role-playing technique. Sales reps are divided into teams of five. When they are ready to start their practice calls, one person does the selling, one is the buyer, one is the discussion leader, and two are observers. Since all teams are working simultaneously, every rep gets to make a practice call even if the total group is a large one.

Before the calls begin, there is a half-hour preparatory session during which each person individually plans a call—either a typical call, or perhaps an actual, difficult call to be made in the near future. Each seller selects the team member to serve as the buyer and gives the buyer an information sheet describing the nature of the call and listing two or three objections the seller wants the buyer to bring up during the call.

The role of the discussion leader is to: (1) caution the buyer if he or she becomes too obnoxious, (2) warn the seller when time allowed for the call (usually 15 or 20 minutes) is nearly up, (3) call on the seller to critique the call first, (4) get the buyer's reaction and comments, (5) ask each observer to comment on what was well handled about the call and only then to suggest possible improvements, and (6) add his or her own comments at the end.

After the critique, the roles rotate among the five team members: there is a new seller, new buyer, new conference leader, and again two observers. After five such periods, everyone has been a seller once, a buyer once, a discussion leader once, and an observer twice.

An alternative view was expressed by Craig Hattabaugh of Aspen Technology: "I'm not afraid of role-playing. I just think it's a waste of time. I think its effectiveness decreases with the complexity of the situation you are trying to simulate. Keep it simple. An entire sales call is very complex. Simulate just a piece of it and then hit the street and practice real time. That's where the learning will happen."

The Motivational Portions

Since first-line sales managers are not selected primarily for their ability to deliver inspirational speeches, they use such devices as the following to generate that "we-can-do-it" atmosphere:

1. Invite a very good customer to explain why he or she likes your product or service much better than that of your competitors.
2. Use an outside inspirational speaker.
3. Rent an inspirational movie or videotape; there are scores of them on the market.

Company Meeting Programs

This section covers meeting programs of specific companies.

Andy Anderson, G. D. Searle:

Our managers run four one-day meetings a year. We give them a plan of action, all the current marketing materials, and a taped message from senior sales management or one of the more senior marketing people at headquarters, but that accounts for only about 40 percent of the meeting. Managers do anything they want with the remaining 60 percent of the time. We do not permit two-day meetings.

The most important thing about the first-line manager's 60 percent is that it be carefully planned. Meetings fall apart when managers don't give enough thought to what their message is going to be, don't prepare their material adequately, don't get themselves good and organized.

We do lots of role-playing in these plan-of-action meetings. We walk through the medical material piece by piece so they all know exactly what it means.

___ lealing with physicians, our reps are frequently challenged and have to have a lot of facts at their fingertips. We do a lot of third-party selling. We'll say, ". . . the blood level is so-and-so, and in this study at Johns Hopkins, Doctor, you will see that . . ." We have to prove ourselves continually.

Each manager has about two hours to cover local issues (in addition to the current literature and activities). Maybe it's a Medicaid situation that's germane to that district, maybe a huge hospital is getting ready to change formularies from one product to another, anything that is localized. They get about three hours of material from us, and the remainder of the time they can bob and weave any way they wish.

Bill Hammick, McKesson Drug Co.:

Our first-line managers run one-day or day-and-a-half sessions at the nearest distribution center. The company supplies the marketing programs, but managers plan and run the meetings themselves. I arrange the agenda. I interview the vendor reps who are scheduled to make short presentations.

The sales meeting is the most important day in the month. It can recharge the batteries of the sales force. If they've had a bad month, this is your chance to rejuice them and get them going. You have to listen to them, review what has happened in the past month, show them how they compare with national results, let them know how they're doing.

We carry 27,000 items, so many things can go wrong. Therefore, early in the meeting, I listen to their problems. The distribution center manager and staff are there, too, to listen to their problems, decide how they'll be handled in the future, and then "let's get on to more important things."

We try to include fifteen minutes or so of "continuing education"— refresher sales training, reminders of sales methods appropriate to a particular marketing program.

Opening new accounts is important. For each rep there is a poster board with the rep's name at the top. At each meeting, the rep writes on the board the names of the new accounts opened in the last month. When a rep who hasn't opened any new accounts sees five or six listed on other reps' boards, that first rep is pretty well motivated to open some new accounts in the coming month.

At the end of the meeting, each rep gets a few minutes to stand up and tell about his or her "success story of the month." I tape them and sometimes distribute an edited tape of the best of them. The reps are limited to one incident, not a lot of them. The reps vote on the best one and that person gets a small prize. So every meeting ends with fifteen different ideas on selling.

Communications Sales Manager:

Because my company is a large Fortune 500 corporation, the sales meeting is an effective tool to ensure that all salespeople are informed of current company programs, policies, and procedures. The objective is to have them concentrate on selling, not worry about rumors.

We conduct Monday morning meetings and one monthly all-day meeting to review current sales results, adjust the sales process, make product announcements, and give briefings on administrative matters. There is a regular topic labeled Rumor Control to address specific issues that are potential roadblocks to selling.

At the weekly meeting one account team is always scheduled to review an open sales situation. The objective is to foster teamwork by soliciting creative solutions from the entire group and sharing the knowledge base of the entire team.

Howard Strelsin, Terminix International:

Each of our branches holds a sales meeting of not more than forty-five minutes one morning each week. The day varies from branch to branch, but each branch always holds its meetings on the same day each week. The division sends suggested outlines to the branch managers. One meeting per month is devoted to sales skills, one to technical product information, and the others are on various subjects.

Jerry McCloskey, Heinz U.S.A.:

District meetings focus on the troops who are called upon to execute the plans of top management. They need this encouragement.

My early training, as all of us have experienced, included many a boring meeting, all the way from the monotone meeting leader who lost his audience after the first hour of an all-day meeting to the fire-and-brimstone speakers who intimidate their troops.

The manager's planning, actions, and procedures become a model for the recruits eager to get the manager's job. At Heinz we have four or five competitors in every category we're in. The goal at a local sales meeting is to exchange information and then establish concise goals and priorities.

Printed outlines of the important topics covered in the meeting are mandatory. Handouts for the reps to use later in the field also work well. I even had a semiannual retail priority goal sheet that was to be placed either on the car visor or in the in-store "brain book."

The agenda must be well organized, but it can be flexible. If one subject becomes too involved, postpone further discussion until later in the meeting. Managers who are comfortable with them can vary the use of slides, overhead projectors, videotapes, and handouts.

A goal of mine was to get interaction from everyone at the meeting. Assignments were given out two weeks in advance to everyone from the newest recruit to the most seasoned veteran. Outside guest speakers from the home office, or marketing specialists, can add a different air to the meeting. It's a good idea to have some gift with the company logo, like a pen or key chain, for everyone at the meeting.

Without browbeating or overdoing it, keep the meeting objectives clear and repeat them from time to time, especially at a two-day meeting.

The team should work and play together from top to bottom, as evidenced by little things such as having the newest rep ride with the boss in the boss's golf cart.

Tim Duncan, American Greetings:

Tim Duncan submitted the following outline of a typical two-day meeting for thirteen sales reps and his assistant:

The objective of the meeting was twofold. First, I needed to create a bond among the reps and install a team spirit instead of the constant competition of one against all. At the time, a great deal of new business was coming into the district, which resulted in a great deal of physical labor to install new fixturing. Up to this point sales reps were reluctant to assist one another because of the loss of time (and sales) in their own territories. Second, the district sales volume had begun to fall behind our previous pace, and we needed a push to regain that pace.

The meeting was held at a very nice resort south of Atlanta that was experiencing a slow period. They were very willing to negotiate an attractive package at a reasonable rate. By doubling up the sales reps as roommates, they had a chance to spend much time together and the meeting fell well within my budget.

The meeting began with a gift for each of the sales reps: a padded folder with their names printed on the front along with the meeting's theme, "Pump Up the Volume." There happened to be a popular song currently on the radio with this theme written in the lyrics, so as the meeting began the song was played in the background.

Each rep was also given an autograph booklet with the names of the other reps typed into it. Each rep was asked to obtain the signatures of all the other reps along with a few sentences about a shared experience or a good wish toward the other rep. When the autograph books were completed at the end of the meeting, they were tossed together and one was randomly selected as the winner of a three-day vacation in the southwestern United States.

The first day's session began with new products and selling strategies. We then role-played in four groups of three as buyers and sellers. Then the teams were alternated and the roles reversed.

The afternoon strategy was built around management techniques that apply to our service personnel. We again divided into groups for role-playing on the subjects we had discussed. The format was slightly different in that the conflicts in the role-play were sequenced and the next one could not be approached until the previous one had been solved. Reps were forced to help one another overcome the conflict, as each had to solve one conflict before going on to the next. By the end of the day, each rep had been on a team with every other rep, helping one another and learning new sales and management techniques.

That evening we divided into three groups to play Wallyball—volleyball played on a racquet ball court. This is a sport in which anyone can be successful regardless of athletic skill or ability. Everyone had a great time and you could see the team spirit really beginning to grow. This was followed by a cocktail reception (a chance to collect autographs) in the hospitality suite that the hotel donated as part of the package. After the reception we had a group dinner.

After dinner everyone returned to the hospitality suite for cocktails and a game of "Win, Lose or Draw." This was a competition of guys against gals, which was a great deal of fun and again required teamwork.

I sensed that the meeting format was working when the game officially stopped at midnight, but the group stayed much longer.

The next morning began again with more theme music and more sales strategies. The last segment of the meeting was spent on bringing the sales reps up-to-date on company activities. We then broke for a group luncheon and an afternoon of recreation—golf, tennis, bike riding, swimming, or hiking. This recreation was furnished by the resort again at no extra fee, as part of the meeting package. Each rep had selected a recreation prior to the meeting and was well prepared for the afternoon.

That evening we met at my assistant's home for a barbecue (he volunteered, of course). The evening ended around 9 o'clock and everyone went home for the weekend.

The months ahead went extremely smoothly. The sales reps helped one another continuously and there was never a disappointment. To this day they are all much better friends, and sales have again improved.

Lori Schweitzer-Teisman, Olsten Temporaries:

We hold eight half-day "brain storming" sessions a year for all account reps. Most sessions run from 12:30 to 4:30 including luncheon. This gives the reps a full morning for selling before heading for the meeting site. Most are held in our corporate office, but one session each year is a full day in a very open, casual setting and one is a Christmas dinner meeting.

Reps take turns planning and conducting the meeting. The agenda is such that everyone participates. The host rep is responsible for providing something relating to training and development, such as a film or article.

Jim Nichols, Dow Chemical USA:

Other meeting ideas include:

1. Joining with other districts to combine ideas on how other sellers tackle their problems.
2. Using company resources such as training managers, personnel managers, credit managers, managers from other functions to describe how those functions operate and how they can help sellers attain their objectives.
3. All meetings should start with the question: "Is the main purpose of this meeting business or pleasure?" and let the answer determine how much time is devoted to each.

Checking Out the Site

The impact of the meeting can be spoiled if the audiovisual props don't work, if there is a noisy meeting in the adjoining conference room, or if any minor details go wrong.

Bob Whyte, retired VP of marketing for Porter Henry & Co., Inc., used the following checklist in making advance arrangements with the conference site (his form has space in which to fill in the details under each topic).

- Name of hotel of conference site
- Key contact
- Meeting rooms (size, acoustics, chairs, lighting, U-shaped layout, round tables, freedom from distraction)
- Breakout rooms (size, proximity, number available)

- A/V equipment (flipcharts, OH projector, carrousel, wireless mike, in-house AV person, local rental, close-circuit TV, podium)
- Hospitality suite arrangements
- Full American plan (group rates, gratuities, advance check-in)
- Welcome cocktail party or dinner arrangements and location
- Recreational arrangements
- Spouses program
- References (recent corporate guests)
- Preregistration
- Gratuities, how handled
- Conference staff availability
- Travel arrangements
- Beverage arrangements (by the bottle? the drink?)
- Security in meeting room (locked at night? Can we leave sheets on wall?)

9

Managing the Manager's Time

In many companies the first-line sales manager faces time demands greater than those on other company executives. Demands on the manager's time come up from the sales force, down from the company, and sideways from customers, industry affairs, and community activities. Yet, often the first-line manager is the only one without full-time secretarial assistance.

This chapter offers ways of managing the first-line manager's time, as suggested by experienced sales managers.

Letting Go of Customers

The newly promoted first-line manager often finds it difficult to avoid spending too much time with former customers (although he or she will maintain contact with higher management of the former customers). In any minor crisis, customers often prefer to phone their former sales rep, who is now the manager, rather than the new sales rep whom they don't know so well.

The manager needs to convince those customers that their requests will actually be handled more quickly if they go directly to the sales rep, rather than involve another layer of people.

"The 'handoff' back to the sales rep can be done very diplomatically by explaining what you are going to do," says Craig Hattabaugh of Aspen Technology. "For example, the manager might say, 'I'm going to ask Joe (the new rep on the account) to dig up that information for you and get it to you before Friday.' "

"When tactfully done, this works well," notes Tim Duncan of American Greetings. "I have explained my new position and responsibilities to the old customers and the fact that their business will be better cared for by the new reps. It also helps to tell them you'll keep an eye out for their businesses. Many new managers believe their replacement isn't as good as they are, and since they know the territory, it's more difficult to let go. Remember, you weren't as good then as you are now. With your training and guidance, the new rep can be just as good as you were. Work with the rep calling on those old customers and difficult accounts and help the rep win the customer's trust as you once did.

"It's difficult for managers to wean old customers once they are promoted. This seems to work better when it is a weaning process and not done in 'cold turkey' fashion. The cold turkey method can result in damaged relationships, lost rapport, and even lost business. It must be done slowly, shifting the responsibility of the call from the manager to the new sales rep.

"As a sales rep I opened a card shop in Nashville, which became our first in the city and a real showcase for us. After eighteen months of developing this business, I was promoted to a field sales manager in Charlotte, North Carolina. The sales rep now in charge of the account had difficulty working with the owner and it seemed I was phoned every time the two of them didn't agree.

"I began by working with the rep at the account in the manner I used when in his position. I shared my philosophy of developing the account's business, which was a fusion of our corporate goal and the owner's goal. On my next visit to Nashville, we worked with the account again and the rep had changed his philosophy more in line with the owner. We also took the owner out to dinner and she seemed very pleased with the service of the sales rep and the increase in sales. When I visited Nashville again, I took the owner to dinner alone and turned my relationship more social than business. The owner then began to respect my position as manager and respected my sales rep's position."

Avoiding Upward Delegation

Sales reps aren't dummies. If they turn in an incomplete report and the manager finishes it for them, there will be more and more incomplete reports. Sales reps are happy to let managers do the work for them if they can get by with it.

The savvy manager is rigorous in bouncing back to the sales rep any chore, however minor, that the sales rep should have done. In some cases it may be easier and faster for the manager to do it, but making the additional effort to shunt it back to the rep will save time in the long run. And, as Craig Hattabaugh points out, reps can be pretty good at upwardly delegating not just reports, but entire job functions.

"Downward delegation can be a problem too," adds Andy Anderson of G. D. Searle. "If the manager has a time problem, it's usually because somebody higher up is dumping too much administrative work on the manager. We expect our managers to be out in the field 80 percent of their time—four days a week—and ordinarily they don't find it difficult to handle their paperwork in the fifth day. If headquarters assigns some time-consuming task to them, they have the right to fight back: 'If I do this, I'll have to take a couple of days from the field.' "

Setting Priorities

Everybody has been told about the importance of ranking activities into A, B, and C categories based upon their importance, and then concentrating on the A jobs. But it's not as simple as it sounds.

More than one manager has been known to say, "I just can't find the time to get out into the field and work with my reps—I have too many more important demands on my time in the office." This is a case of assigning the wrong priorities. Fieldwork should be an A priority, not a B or C.

Another mistake is the tendency to rank too many functions as A's. Ask a first-line manager to list all the functions he or she is expected to perform. Let's say there are twenty-five items on the list. Then ask the manager to rank them by the A–B–C method. Too often the manager will come up with something like fifteen A's, eight B's, and two C's.

That manager is simply considering too many functions as A priority jobs. A good mental exercise for first-line managers is to list all those functions, then give the A rating to only 15 percent of them, the B rating to about 20 percent, and C to all the rest. This forces the manager to look at the relative importance of all those tasks formerly considered equally important.

Rob McCoy of GTE agrees with the importance of setting priorities and making fieldwork an A. "But," he points out, "priorities change and must be constantly re-evaluated. This is best done by means of short-term planning. Break down plans by those for the quarter, month, week, and day. This helps keep priorities in perspective and allows for change when needed. Take a look at the upcoming quarter about a month in advance, plan for the coming month during the third week of the preceding month, and so on."

Keeping a Time Log—Just Once

Most of us don't have an accurate idea of how our time is really spent. When asked what percentage of their time they spent on each major task and then asked to keep track of their time for a week, managers will often make initial estimates that are off by 100 percent or more.

The jobs we hate to do seem to take up more time than they actually do. If we enjoy doing something, it often takes up more of our time than we realize.

Much as most managers hate paperwork, it will pay them to keep track of their time in fifteen-minute intervals during one typical week. If this is done just once a year, it will give them a clearer picture of their time management problem.

Use a form like that shown in Figure 9-1. Use a two- or three-letter code for listing tasks: TS for telephoning sales reps, TH for telephoning headquarters, and so on. Don't list all paperwork under one category like P; break it down into components like RR for reading reports, WR for writing reports, GC for general correspondence. Many fifteen-minute intervals will be devoted to more than one task; just charge the entire interval to the task that took up most of that time.

Then add up the amount of time spent on each function. What functions are taking up more time than they should? Which should be getting more time? What percentage of time is spent on the A, B, and C functions?

Controlling the Time Eaters

Possible ways of reducing the time spent on some of the C chores include:

• *Combine them.* Do two chores at once. When making a number of phone calls, read sales reports or trade magazines while waiting for the requested person to come to the phone. Handle paperwork while on a plane.

"I can get some paperwork done during long auto rides while working with a rep," says Rob McCoy. "It works best when you can share some of the work with the rep. They enjoy giving input (although you don't always have to use it). You can read aloud and share information from office communications or trade journals."

• *Set a time limit.* Decide that Job X is worth only Y minutes and drop it at the end of that time. A certain business publication, for

Figure 9-1. Sample time log form.

WEEKLY TIME LOG

Week of _____

CODE

CS = Corres, sales   RR = Reading reports   CFS = Conf, sales rep
CH = Corres, HQ   RG = Reading, general   CFH = Conf, HQ
CM = Corres, misc   T   = Travel   WR   = Writing reports
                         SCA = Sales call alone
                         SCW = Sales call with sales rep

ETC—DESIGN YOUR OWN CODES

	Mon	Tues	Wed	Thur	Fri	Sat/Sun
8:00–9:00						
9:00–9:15						
9:15–9:30						
9:30–9:45						
9:45–10:00						
10:00–10:15						
10:15–10:30						
10:30–10:45						
10:45–11:00						
11:00–11:15						
11:15–11:30						
11:30–11:45						
11:45–12:00						
12:00–1:00						
1:00–1:15						
1:15–1:30						
1:30–1:45						
1:45–2:00						
2:00–2:15						
2:15–2:30						
2:30–2:45						
2:45–3:00						
3:00–3:15						
3:15–3:30						
3:30–3:45						
3:45–4:00						
4:00–4:15						
4:15–4:30						
4:30–4:45						
4:45–5:00						
Evening						

Note that 8:00–9:00, 12:00–1:00, and Evening are longer than the other 15-minute intervals.

example, may be worth no more than ten minutes. Learn to skim it in ten minutes. If there's a long article you want to read, set it aside for a later time—maybe during one of those plane rides mentioned above.

◆ *Bunch similar jobs.* Some chores that consume considerable time when handled one by one can be accomplished in much less total time if they are accumulated and then handled in a batch.

◆ *Delegate.* This doesn't necessarily mean you need to have an assistant. Are you doing something the sales reps could do for you? Are you compiling some kind of information your company might be able to provide?

"Delegation is an excellent way to control time," adds Robert McCoy of GTE. "I gladly delegate to a rep any project, or any research for a project, that's within their realm of responsibility. This motivates the reps and they give it their best. I also ensure that they get credit for their work, and this gives them additional exposure to upper management. Delegated assignments also break the monotony of routine daily work. Our reps handle a wide variety of work anyway, but this adds additional excitement."

◆ *Find a shortcut.* A phone call is faster than writing a memo or letter (even if it is faxed!).

Some of our participants offer further advice:

Communications Sales Manager:

Work habits and work styles are very individualistic. Since most sales managers were salespeople before, they have developed their unique ways of handling the priorities of their company and their customers.

The most important skill I have developed is to take the first ninety minutes of the day to complete all required reading and paperwork. My required administrative and planning activities are completed by 8:30 A.M., and after that my style of management is "open door." But meanwhile, virtually one full business day a week has been devoted to administration.

Rob McCoy, GTE:

Time demands are especially excessive if the manager doesn't have a secretary. Some time-saving tips I've used successfully in the past:

1. Use a quality typing service that is near the office and that can

transcribe from compact cassettes. The manager can dictate correspondence at any time and mail or drop off the cassettes. It's helpful to use a service that uses word processing and will keep your files on disk for possible editing and reprinting in the future.

2. Set up a letter-tray filing system that makes sense, for example, by sales rep, customer, headquarters. After you're finished with a piece of paper, toss it into the appropriate tray. On a quarterly basis you can file them away in your file cabinet so you'll know where it is when you need to retrieve it.

3. Touch each piece of paper only once. Take care of most paperwork immediately. If it's a long project, file it in a folder and place it in your briefcase to work on when you have more time for it.

4. Car phones are really helpful. Many calls I used to make at work I now do on the way to and from the office or a customer, leaving more time for paperwork at the office. Before leaving on a flight, instead of rushing to make the calls at the office and then speeding to the airport, I now leave for the airport earlier and make the calls on the way.

5. I do some paperwork in my hotel room on about half my nights on the road. I have a small office kit (stapler, paper clips, tape, and such) in my garment bag that I use for this work. I know some managers who carry a second brief case for hotel room paperwork.

6. In dealing with time management, don't forget the "big picture" priorities: family, with a bit of time just for yourself, and your work and your career.

The last thought on this subject that works well for me is Do It Now. The best way to save time later is to do it now, don't procrastinate. Companies tend to generate a lot of paperwork. If you don't stay on top of it by using all possible methods to Do It Now, you fall far behind and become less effective as an administrator and manager.

Jerry McCloskey, Heinz U.S.A.:

A manager's time is an asset that can't be wasted. The good manager knows that he or she must learn to juggle multiple tasks instead of concentrating on a few key ones.

First-line managers need to focus their time on their main duty: selling. The trap many fall into is the process of reinventing the wheel on reports and forms for their people and spending more time on administration than is necessary. Sales are rarely made in the manager's home or office.

There are many systems—mental ways of organizing physical binders, folders, files, index cards—that are a habit with most businesspeople. Your day doesn't start with a buzzer. Thoughts, plans, and to-do lists should be reviewed at the end of each day so that time can be used efficiently the next day.

Jack Woods, United States Cellular:

Time management begins with learning to say no tactfully. Much as you'd like to say yes to every request from every person every moment, you need to prioritize and say no when necessary.

Dave Singer, Cellular One:

Managing your time becomes increasingly important as your span of control is increased. I find it helpful to write down my plans for the next thirty days so I can visualize them and share this information with my team so they know what my priorities are.

10

Slumps and Plateaus

A slump is a period during which a sales rep's productivity drops far below its expected level. A plateau is that phenomenon when a sales rep—usually, but not necessarily, an older one—simply "tops off" and produces far below his or her potential.

With younger reps, Alina Bilodeau of The Clorox Company points out that "learning curves flatten out. It's important for the manager to sense this and for the rep to report it. I always encourage the SRs to communicate with me. We plan their careers jointly, but personal accountability for their own actions and career will make them successful."

Slumps

Almost every sales rep runs into one of them, now and then. What can the first-line manager do about them?

Spot Them Early

The manager who receives sufficiently up-to-date sales figures can usually observe the symptoms early enough to check a slump in its early stages.

"Slumps must be watched," comments Jerry McCloskey of Heinz U.S.A. "Checkpoints can monitor those things that do happen. Examples are reports on weekly or monthly sales results, account profiles, dollar rankings, distribution checks, and field reports. First-line and middle management should be sensitive to every shift in the trend of a brand. Problems should be discussed openly and not be kept quiet until it is too late to correct a negative trend."

Olsten Temporaries of Cincinnati matches performance versus projects to detect slumps, reports Lori Schweitzer-Teismann. "We have the account representatives project what their top clients will produce in dollar sales during the following year. These projections are set up on spreadsheets and year-to-date totals added quarterly. In this way slumps can be spotted quickly, discussed, and hopefully resolved."

When a rep's productivity is below target for two or three report periods, the manager simply phones to ask the rep, "What's the problem? What can we do to help you?"

It may be that the disappointing results are caused by some external factor, totally beyond the control of the individual seller. If that's the case, the sooner the manager identifies the problem, the better.

Analyze the Causes

Sometimes a clue to the cause can be found in the sales reports themselves. If the rep is not making enough calls, the answer may lie in a revision of work habits: working hours, routing, doing nonselling work in the evenings.

If the rep is making calls but not seeing enough decision makers, the need is for training in making appointments and handling receptionists.

If the rep is seeing enough of the right people but not getting the orders, we're back to coaching on sales techniques—assuming that there is no external cause such as a change in the market or in competitive activity.

"Reps sometimes fall behind in production because they don't realize how much time is lost during the year to vacations, legal holidays, company meetings, training sessions, and other nonselling activities," notes Dave Singer of Cellular One. "If a rep needs to sell 100 widgets a year and sets a target of two per week, the rep will end up about 25 percent below quota because of this time loss."

"A manager should be on the lookout for personal problems and temporary family setbacks as reasons for the field rep's being distracted and not assume that the seller's effectiveness or performance is lacking or in need of attention," is the reminder from Jim Nichols of Dow Chemical. "Under these circumstances the sellers may simply need a little understanding by their managers until they work their way through whatever is distracting them in their personal lives. If a company is to demand loyalty and dedication, it should be prepared to give it as well. All the company's employees are going to have some sort of personal distractions somewhere in their lifetimes or careers, and a company should be prepared to deal with that in a sympathetic and cooperative manager. The result will be greater loyalty from the employee and better performance in the long run."

"Be sure you receive sales reports on time," notes Lori Teismann. "A slump is sometimes evident when paperwork starts getting behind—could the rep be in such a slump that he or she is lumping two weeks worth of calls on one weekly report to make it appear that goals are being met? Have reps turn in weekly itineraries and question any appointments that don't appear on sales reports.

"Make sure reps are caught up on their record keeping. If they're behind in their correspondence and sales records, the slump may be caused by a feeling of being overwhelmed. In this case, ask the rep how much time off from sales calls he or she needs to get caught up with paperwork so they can again concentrate on effective selling. The manager may need to show the rep how to handle paperwork more efficiently—and also to make sure that not too many nonselling chores have been delegated to the rep."

"Look real closely at the rep who appears to be in a slump," says Tom Dunning of Datacard Corp., "and if the rep is doing the right things, show the rep that you have confidence in him or her. Encourage the rep to keep going."

Alex Jones of Allstate Insurance Co. advises: "Distinguish between the productive rep in a temporary slump and the everyday poor performer. People don't just hit dead periods; dead periods are a deliberate act, usually the failure to do things that are important. Sit down with the rep, lay out the facts—which means you need to have the pertinent information to show the rep how bad the slump is. Bad habits can sneak up on a person. The rep tells himself, 'I had a bad week last week' and next week 'I had a cold' and next week something else went wrong. Show the rep the record over the last six months compared to last month.

"Ask the rep, 'What were you doing when you were producing at this level? What are you not doing now that you were doing then?'

"You need to have regular checkpoint meetings with all individual reps. Praise them for what they're doing well, find out if they can do better, are they still satisfied with the goals they set or should they be raised, and if their strategies aren't reaching their goals, should their strategies be changed?

"With the habitual poor performer, there's only one way to work and that is to have a corrective or disciplinary plan. Let the rep know that he or she is not working up to their goals or to your expectations. Look for some form of short-term improvement, and when you reach that move on to the next level. But when you start this corrective action, make it clear that the rep is either going to improve or be terminated. No sense stringing the rep along."

A different approach is taken by Andy Anderson of G. D. Searle: "If you have the right kinds of field managers, the reps don't go into slumps," he points out. "If you see two or three slumped reps in one district, take a look at the manager and ask what's going on there.

"The manager will first counsel the rep and tell him or her about the slump and give the rep a prescribed program to help him or her get out of it. Most of the slumped reps you can save come out of it that way.

"If it continues and we think the rep is worth saving, we might bring him or her into the home office for a regeneration program—let the rep see the building, talk to people, remember how it was when he or she first started.

"If that doesn't work, we put the rep on a ninety-day probationary program. We apply a lot of heat and say that if things don't turn around quickly—'here's the prescribed course of action I want you to take and we'll measure you against it in ninety days . . .'

"We can measure the rep's performance by dollar sales and on the products we're promoting we have a prescription count at the territory level.

"If you lay down a philosophy of measurement, it makes managing very easy, because you simply say to the person, 'I know you may be working hard, but the cold hard facts are that you're not putting the scores on the scoreboard, and what options do I have?'

"I'm a strong believer in a strong budget philosophy. The budget is the one thing you can't lie out of around here.

"Poor first-line management is the biggest cause of slumps. In 90 percent of the cases, it's the manager who's letting the rep get careless, isn't keeping the rep challenged, isn't keeping the rep motivated.

"We have one rep on a probationary program. I changed managers there about two months ago and the rep is going like a rocket right now. I know it's because the manager is giving him some attention and respect. I think the first-line manager is everything."

"Slumps happen frequently," says Bill Hammick of McKesson Drug Co. "First thing I do is phone the rep and say, 'There are a few things here that are a little disturbing—tell me about it.' If I can't get a specific answer, I'll say 'Let's have breakfast and talk it over.' You can almost always uncover the reason for a slump—a personal problem, or perhaps something the company did that irked the rep. The last thing I want is a sales rep out there with something gnawing on him that's creating a lack of performance. A negative attitude can wreck performance."

"Frequent field visits are a must," says Jerry McCloskey of Heinz U.S.A. "A sales manager cannot be knowledgeable about market conditions without periodic trips to where it is happening. Of course, first-line and middle sales management should make it their job to be out with the accounts and their people."

Schedule Field Visits

In any event, it's important for the manager to get out into the field and spend a day or so working with the rep. This bolsters the rep's morale by showing that the boss and the company are behind him or her.

In conversations that are helpful rather than critical, the manager can encourage the rep to analyze the problem. On sales calls, the manager can demonstrate selling methods or can observe the rep's techniques and offer helpful suggestions.

"Pump up your people on these trips," says Jerry McCloskey. "Ask questions, give them praise if they deserve it, and call a spade a spade if poor performance is seen. Share ideas, be creative, relate experiences in other markets, and above all leave the rep with a commitment to attain some specific objective as a result of the time you spent with him or her. Many field people think no one really knows or cares about their situation.

"When a good rep is in a slump and losing confidence in him- or herself, that's a good time to go back to step one and work in the field with the rep. If you make sales, great! You show them some success; if you fail, they see that you can fail too. Meanwhile you've shown them that you're interested in them, that you still believe in them, that a temporary slump doesn't mean you've lost confidence in them."

"Take the rep aside," says D. M. House of NCR, "and say, 'We recognize that you're in a slump. Everyone gets in a slump now and then. What you need to do is to ask yourself, Am I doing everything, everyday, the way I know how to do it? If I keep doing that, I know the sales will come.' The worst thing a rep can do is to worry about the situation and start pressing, because the customer can sense a sales rep who is pressing."

"Identify the factors causing the slump, such as poor closing," advises Howard Strelsin of Terminix International. "First, get the rep's interpretation of what he or she perceives to be the problem. Second, call customers who didn't buy and ask them why they didn't. Branch managers have a lost sales checklist of questions to ask. Maybe the customer couldn't see the differences between our services and lower-priced ones. Third, observe calls to see what the rep is doing. Fourth, everyone who hits a slump has had a previous peak. Ask the rep to recall what he or she was doing when selling well. Slumps often result from the rep taking shortcuts, like the home run hitter failing to touch second."

Set Interim Goals

One way to restore the rep's morale is to set some short-term and partial goals that the rep can almost certainly accomplish.

"Let's temporarily forget our long-term goal of selling across the board," the manager might say. "For the next week or so, just concentrate on Product Y and get those sales up to par."

Demonstrate the Law of Averages

Sales reps sometimes misinterpret the law of averages as an excuse for making poor calls, feeling that "if I make enough of them, the law of averages will give me some sales." This rep forgets that his average will be a lot better if he concentrates on making the best possible sales presentation on each call.

But in many types of selling, there is a random factor. Just as a tossed coin may occasionally come up tails five times in a row, so the best of sellers will almost certainly hit a streak of disappointing results.

To prevent reps from being discouraged by such a run of failures, one manager used this demonstration at a sales meeting:

"Don't let runs of unsuccessful calls get you down, any more than a run of successful calls should encourage you to slack off.

"Let's say that on the average you make one sale every three calls. Here's a deck of cards. I've taken out the spades. Let's say the thirteen clubs represent successful sales, and the twenty-six red cards represent no sales. Now I'll shuffle this deck very thoroughly and deal the cards. Watch what happens."

What happens is that at times there will be long runs of discouraging red cards. At other times, black cards will come up more frequently than expected.

"Don't let either of these runs persuade you to do anything but your best on every call," the manager observes. "And also notice that, by improving your sales skills, you'll increase the odds in your favor— just like stuffing the deck with more black cards."

When a rep is discouraged by a run of unsuccessful calls, Alina Bilodeau of Clorox sets up some "pushover" calls without the rep being aware of it.

"The net effect is a more confident and motivated salesperson as a result of the sting of success," she reports. "After each call, positive aspects as well as areas for improvement are carefully discussed."

n reps are in a slump, we put them through a videotaping session," reports David Ruckman of Merrill Lynch. "Get four or five of them in a room and let them watch their own presentations on video. In a way it's training, but after they've done it two or three times it's a great confidence builder because they refine their presentations and see themselves making an effective presentation on tape. They say, 'Gee, I do that pretty well.' "

The Plateaued Sales Rep

In practically every mature and stable sales force, there are some sales reps—and some first-line managers—who are simply not doing as well as they could be.

Usually they were very bright and promising at the beginning of their sales (or sales management) careers, but they reached a point at which they seem to be just going through the motions.

It is a problem that perplexes many companies and is not solved by exposing the plateaued persons to motivational films or inspirational speakers.

There are two basic causes for this resting-on-the-oars attitude (although the plateaued persons themselves may not be aware of them): (1) they have no pressing need for more money, and (2) they're bored with their jobs.

We might be able to eliminate the first cause if we could get the plateaued sales rep to desire a yacht, or a Rolls Royce, or a much bigger home. Assuming the rep is compensated in proportion to sales results, the rep would have to pour on the steam to achieve the goal.

But usually it's more practical to tackle the second cause. How can we make the job more challenging? Companies have been able to reinvigorate plateaued sellers by making them responsible for a difficult new product introduction, or for key accounts, or for some other challenging assignment.

Alina Bilodeau of Clorox reports that "in setting up yearly business projections, I encourage reps to set short-term career objectives, analyze their strengths and weaknesses, identify projects they'd like to work on, even set personal goals. This has a sublime effect on productivity."

Howard Strelsin, Terminix International:

The plateaued sales rep is in his or her "comfort zone." The rep may appear very eager and motivated during the application interview, but later you find that the spouse is making a good income and the rep doesn't care much whether his or her income is a few dollars more or less. The rep doesn't want to work harder, make the extra calls, making evening appointments, work on Saturdays.

One way to avoid this problem is to interview the spouse before hiring. How hungry will the rep be? Also ask yourself, "Is it a behavioral problem or a skill problem?" If behavioral, look for some personal problem that is demotivating the rep.

Jim Nichols, Dow Chemical USA:

The subject of the plateaued salesperson is very complex. The manager is unlikely to be able to motivate the seller to want a yacht or Rolls Royce and should confine his or her efforts to providing professional challenge to the field seller. The manager can control the level of difficulty of the job and the recognition available to the seller on a professional basis. The manager can change the field seller's assignment to provide variety. The manager can add new responsibilities that focus the energies of the field seller in an area where the seller has some particular talent and interest in demonstrating his or her capabilities. Or the manager can provide additional training that may round out a seller's capabilities and shore up an area of weakness. I believe the manager should concentrate efforts in those areas, and those areas alone.

There are a variety of things that can be done to provide challenge in the job, such as encouraging monitoring activities with new field sellers, demonstrating a particular knowledge of an industry or marketplace that can be used by the company in determining marketing programs. We sometimes include the field seller as a temporary member of product or business teams when the seller has a particular contribution to make. This both compliments the seller and helps the business with some real-life field input.

D. M. House, NCR:

When you get somebody for whom sales are rolling in, I remind the rep that the easiest time in the world to get an order is when you have one in your pocket. When you're running ahead of quota you're loose, you're thorough, and that's the time when you make money. This is what you're after. The only way to hit top earnings is to make sales while sales are good. In our company, our commissions increase after we have achieved our quotas.

If things are too easy for them and they're not working their terrorities properly, you might consider that they have too much territory and give a piece of it to a hungrier rep.

Tom Dunning, Datacard Corp.:

If an effective sales rep gets satisfied wuth underachieved results, if the rep's a top talent you're depending upon for production and is at a pleateau level, you can cut the territory so the rep has to work harder to get his or her income back up to what it was. The downside of that is that the rep may leave. You have to evaluate that possibility. But if you have a fat-cat sales rep sitting on a big territory and working three hours a day, the other sales reps are aware of it and it's terrible for morale.

Alex Jones, Allstate Insurance:

With the fat cat, you have to find a way to convince the rep, without the rep thinking it's your idea, that he or she wants to do better. You look for ways to sow the seed in this person's mind that he wants to accomplish something he hasn't yet accomplished, reach a goal that hasn't been reached. He wants to buy a mountaintop cabin or a new boat or whatever the case may be.

People will not do what you want them to do; they will strive only for their own personal goals. They don't give a damn about what I want to accomplish.

People will not work harder just to make more money. That's a fact of life. But if you can plant some dream in their mind, they'll work harder for that.

At a quarterly review session with a career rep who's not doing as well as he should, I'll say, "There's a book that hasn't yet been written, and that's about the career sales rep who doesn't want to get into management. What motivates that rep to keep doing well?" What I'm really trying to find out is what motivates this particular rep. Often he's going through a phase in which he wonders if he shouldn't have gone into management, is gloomily looking forward to another fifteen years in the field. You have to make him feel important. Maybe you can find him temporary assignment in some other type of work, like training; usually they're glad to get back into the field.

Factors Affecting Slumps and Plateaus

"A major problem that senior salespeople often have," says Rob McCoy of GTE, "is that they, over time, find creative ways to shortcut the sales process in order to gain efficiency. Sometimes this catches up with them and reduces their efficiency, but they can't see what's happened because it came about gradually. Refresher seminars, particularly with outside groups or consultants, can be very helpful in getting the rep back on the track, both skillwise and emotionally.

"A great way to deal with these situations is to bring the sales team into play to support the problem salesperson both technically and emotionally. (This assumes that the manager has built a team that supports its members.) Sales meetings and rallies can serve as a platform for the team to work on the problem.

"A way to avoid both slumps and plateaus is to stay close to the rep on a continuing basis. Regular work plan reviews, sales visits, and field coaching will serve this purpose very well.

"Don't try to apply generalized solutions. Do good diagnostics and apply sound solutions at the individual and human level—assuming, of course, that there is a solid rapport as a basis for this."

Says the Communications Sales Manager, "You can never lose focus on the target, and the target is to generate and maintain sales for the organization. This is a never-ending battle and can be stimulated by material posted in the office and not getting yourself caught in a rut.

"The sales manager must always demonstrate this in every aspect of the job: coaching, administrative work, company functions, recognition events, community events, and so on. You need to establish and maintain a results-oriented organization if you are to be successful. These fundamentals must be understood by every member of the organization and universally maintained.

"On an individual basis, it is imperative to know what the salesperson's individual objectives are and to always work toward helping him or her to achieve them. As a rule, salespeople (and their managers) have large egos and varying objectives. By understanding each of their respective desires, you have to demonstrate your desire for them to succeed. These objectives can be either horizontal growth with the organization, vertical advancement, community interests, education, location, family, recreation, religion, lifestyle, and so on. Individual plans must be jointly developed and implemented with continuous feedback.

"By keeping these two fundamental approaches in place, it is the exception when a slump or plateau is reached because there is constant two-way communication always stressing the individual objectives and sales role expectations."

11

Fire Fighting
and Troubleshooting

The reps out in the field are bound to encounter an occasional question, problem, or big opportunity that they can't handle themselves and have to buck up the line to their sales manager. The goal of the manager is to make these emergencies as infrequent as possible.

When a sales rep is initially promoted to first-line management, it's sometimes difficult to let go of former customers. When a customer wants a price break, a better delivery schedule, or some other favor, instead of turning to the newly assigned and relatively unknown sales rep, the customer will often make a long-distance call to his old friend and golfing chum who has now been promoted to manager.

If the manager handles inquiries that could just as well have been handled by the rep, that takes valuable time away from more important duties. So the manager tries to "wean" the customer away from the manager and to the new sales rep.

The manager, of course, never implies that he or she is too busy to do a favor for an old friend. Instead, the new manager convinces the customer that action will be faster by referring problems to the sales rep.

"I'd like to help you out," the manager explains, "but Newseller has all the records. She's right on top of everything in the district. I'll have her phone you."

There will, of course, be problems the manager must handle because they're simply outside the knowledge or authority of the field rep. In these cases the manager does everything possible to enhance the importance of the sales rep. For example, he may tell the customer that the answer to a difficult problem was suggested by the rep.

If the manager encounters too many of these emergencies, a good question to wrestle with is, "Why *can't* the sales rep be given the authority to handle this type of problem?"

Some specific comments from sales managers:

Andy Anderson, G. D. Searle:

Managers tend to do too much fire fighting. A lot of them have trouble making the transition from rep to manager, which really tells you something about your training program. We bring the newly appointed SMs in for nine weeks, which helps a bit in divorcing them from the field.

The keys are awareness and training. It's strictly a matter of delegation and not being a savior. The manager can say to the rep, "You got yourself into this mess, here are some ideas and suggestions. But unless it's a huge account of a very influential person, I don't intend to come out and pull your ass out of these things."

The situation is much the same as with kids who get into trouble—you bail them out the first time and after that you let them know that they're on their own. It's really a business judgment.

If the manager does have to intervene personally, it's okay to make the action a training experience so it doesn't have to be repeated. In a very tough postcall session, the manager tells the rep, "I bailed you out of this one, but it's the last one."

If reps realize they can get away with passing the buck enough times, they'll collect problems and when the manager goes out to work with the rep, the day will be spent fire fighting.

Dave Singer, Cellular One:

It's too easy for a salesperson and a sales manager to get into a constant fire-fighting mode. Be prepared to let some things burn to the ground. However, some fires can represent a tremendous business opportunity. Just imagine that you're selling fire extinguishers.

If the same rep is constantly phoning you about local fires, ask the rep to bunch all the inquiries and phone you at a specific time, such as 7 A.M.

Jack Woods, United States Cellular:

Some fires can get out of control if not handled immediately. Nip them in the bud to avoid wrestling with a major problem later on.

Rob McCoy, GTE:

Direct involvement of sales management with customers can be an important aspect of the job in some customer segments, such as national accounts and other large customers. Details of the sales manager's involvement need to be worked out on a case basis between the sales manager, the customer, and the account executive.

The sales manager needs to champion the needs of the customer (and therefore the account executive) back into his firm. There need to be clear channels and links for dealing with unique situations across functions and departments. Today's competitive markets forbid absolute standardization of product, delivery, and so on. So the sales organization has to have means of customizing. The key is to manage the optimal balance between standards and exceptions.

Alina Bilodeau, The Clorox Company:

Often the problem lies with the buyer. When I was first promoted from a sales rep to an account manager, my first buyer took issue with my company, saying that he was not a "training ground" and resented being given a "young, inexperienced female."

My supervisor was forced into a meeting with the buyer and negotiated a finite time period during which I would have to prove myself and win the buyer's respect and willingness to work with me, regardless of my tenure, age, or sex.

Within a short period, the buyer and I developed an excellent working relationship. I understood his point of view, and instead of being resentful I worked extra hard to win him over. It worked. He turned out to be a good friend as well as an excellent trainer. He took me under his wing and felt he could train and develop me. I helped increase our mutual business, finishing the year at plus 7 percent. What a turnaround!

D. M. House, NCR:

A fire-fighting call is a great opportunity to show a newer salesperson how to handle such problems—in a personal meeting with the customer, never on the phone. Use a letter only to confirm the actions to be taken. Let the salesperson do the follow-up. It will put the rep in good stead with the buyer and take the manager out of this (and future!) situations.

Jim Nichols, Dow Chemical USA:

In almost all cases the rep should be part of the solution to any problem regardless of how it was brought to the attention of the manager. Sometimes the customer just wants to interact with management and should be allowed to do so on a direct basis. The manager in these cases must be capable of walking the fine line of having a dialogue with the customer while not undercutting the influence of the sales rep. Good reps usually recognize that their customers need to have a relationship with company management and create situations in a coordinating way that keeps the field seller as the quarterback in any situation involving the customer and the rep's management.

Tim Duncan, American Greetings:

There are basically two categories of troubleshooting or fire fighting that constantly seem to arise and that a sales rep cannot handle alone: situations that can "add to" business and situations that can "take away" from business.

In either event it is extremely important that the sales representative handle the call. The added support of the sales manager's presence may suffice, or the situation may escalate to the point where it is necessary for the sales manager to become directly involved. When this occurs, it is again important that the sales manager's input is precise and to the point and always turned back over to the sales rep. Short of losing business (and sometimes even this can be expendable to teach a valuable lesson in personnel development), it must appear that the sales rep is in control of the call. Once that is lost, so is the rep's confidence and respect. If this occurs more than once, you can bet your customer will always call you instead of your rep.

Recently my rep had been prospecting a small chain of variety stores supplied by a competitor. He had made a great deal of progress with the chain and had obtained an appointment with the president. I assisted him in the writing of the presentation and about two weeks after that we made the call together. I told the rep I was there only for support, but if he really needed my input he should touch his earlobe.

He did very well at the beginning of the call but got into trouble about the disposal of the competitor's inventory currently in the store. As he began to flounder a bit, he did not touch his ear and I was amazed that he wanted to handle this on his own. Finally the customer began to show signs of frustration at my sales rep's avoiding a direct answer to his question, so then the rep gave me the sign by touching his ear (by the way, I wasn't going to wait much longer; he was in trouble).

I explained our company's policy on this matter and then suggested that his stores follow a procedure this sales rep had used before. It entailed a markdown of the product with support from us to provide inventory depletion with a protection of the store's gross margin, simultaneously building customer goodwill by passing the savings along to them. My sales rep immediately picked up the hint, carried the rest of the call, and closed the sale.

In another situation, another of my sales reps had been contacted by one of her accounts and told that one of our competitors had made a great offer for the business, which the store was going to accept unless she came up with a good reason for them not to change suppliers.

I met with the rep before our appointment, and we brainstormed our position to see what we could do to save the business. She realized that in this case a one-for-one matching of our competitor's terms would not suffice, so negotiation was needed.

As we got into the call, she handled the situation well but began to buckle as the pressure intensified. I was forced to jump in and, as I expected, once I had intervened no one would let me stop until every issue was resolved. The only way I could keep my sales rep involved was to ask her opinion and try to lead the conversation back in her direction. It was basically a successful call, but you just can't win them all.

In fire fighting and troubleshooting, my best advice would be to *always* include your sales rep in each facet of the process. This way they learn by experiencing a "hands-on" situation that allows the manager to delegate some of the responsibility, avoiding the time required to complete the task alone.

Jerry McCloskey, Heinz U.S.A.:

The newer rep's ability to handle the high-stakes situations can be developed at sales meetings by letting others relate their experiences and by using role-playing, case studies, and other methods to develop appropriate strategies.

Major sales opportunities should be documented and communicated to all parties who will have some part in the sale. Each level of management must know what is happening and must "think like the buyer" to anticipate key objections and successful solutions.

Craig Hattabaugh, Aspen Technology:

Don't be afraid to get involved once in a while. It's good to keep in touch with the realities of the trenches.

Determine whether the trouble represents a learning opportunity. If time permits, use "fires" as a means of training your people.

Once in a while salespeople will bump something up to you because they are lazy. Normally you send these back down, but handling one for the rep once in a while helps boost morale.

12

Personal Problems of the Sellers

To what extent should the first-line sales manager be concerned about the individual problems of the sales reps who report to the manager?

There are two sides to this question. On the one hand, we have our innate respect for the privacy of the individual, often expressed as "so long as what the seller is doing doesn't affect performance on the job, it's none of the manager's business." On the other hand, we know that one of the strongest motivating factors is the rep's feeling that the manager really takes deep personal interest in his or her goals, achievements, and problems.

The manager who is really interested in the sales force probably knows this information about each sales rep:

- Spouse's name
- Number and approximate ages of children
- Rep's college (and perhaps college fraternity or sorority)
- Sports engaged in
- Hobbies
- Goals

Some sales managers feel that the manager should never get involved in personal problems of the rep. For example, Tim Duncan of American Greetings says, "After working with the reps, sometimes quite closely, it is difficult not to get involved with their problems. But don't. As sales managers we are not trained to offer counseling on personal problems. Our advice is just a guess, and if it's wrong we can get the rep into deeper trouble. The other danger is that the manager may become so involved in the problem that the manager becomes part of the problem. The best advice is to stay at a distance, be empathetic, and suggest where to get help rather than trying to be the help."

Some managers suggest that there are two occasions when the manager interferes in the rep's personal life: when job performance is affected and when the rep or a member of the rep's family asks for assistance or advice.

Job Performance

Job performance can be affected in subtle ways, as Craig Hattabaugh of Aspen Technology points out. "Most managers can see it but don't have the guts to take issue with it. They hope the problem will solve itself. You can't take issue with personal life, but you can and must take issue with deficient job performance."

"What reps do in their personal time is their own business, as long as it isn't illegal and doesn't affect their work," summarizes Howard Strelsin of Terminix International. "If it affects their work, the manager must try to find out what the problem is. Terminix has a personnel department that is willing to meet a rep halfway if the rep recognizes that he or she has a substance abuse problem and comes to us with it. For example, we will pay some of the costs of Alcoholics Anonymous."

"As soon as the rep's personal problems hit the job, you have to talk about it," agrees Andy Anderson of G. D. Searle. "You don't get involved in it, but simply say, 'Fred, your performance is dropping, there must be some reason for it.' If the rep mentions a marriage problem (they usually don't mention a drug or alcohol problem), the manager can be very direct about requiring a change in behavior. Once the manager has related the problem to job performance, the manager can offer help, but the manager must stick strictly to effects on performance."

"Act only on performance symptoms!" stresses Rob McCoy of GTE. "Don't get personally involved in the problem and try to solve it yourself, but get the employee to professional help."

"The manager should be aware of any inconsistent or 'strange' behavior that could signal a change in the seller's life style or personal situation. The manager should focus his or her concern on the effect on job performance resulting from this change.

"The manager should never try to tackle the personal problem head-on, but should point out to the employee that the resultant behavior is affecting his job performance and suggest that the employee seek professional counseling. In these cases the manager should have some suggestions on persons or organizations the employee might want to contact."

"Listen cautiously when the rep tells you about his or her problems," advises Jack Woods of US Cellular. "Be careful not to say anything inappropriate—it might come back to haunt you. If the problem is affecting performance, have the rep seek professional help through the company's employee assistance program if there is one, or through outside resources."

"Personal problems of any employee—not just sales reps—are difficult situations for everyone concerned," says Craig Hattabaugh of Aspen Technology. "If personal problems are affecting job performance, sales managers may be reluctant to raise the issue, fearing they will add to the employee's burden. This is the wrong approach.

"If you suspect personal trouble, verify it by asking the employee, 'How are things going?' 'Is there anything we can help you with?' If conditions do not improve, assemble the facts and present them in the form: 'Here is what I see happening, this is why it's substandard, and if we can't work together to fix it here is what will happen.' My experience has been that this 'wake-up call' has a very positive long-term impact, although it is every tough to deliver."

Assistance and Advice

"My experience is that people will not seek help until a loss—a job, a family member—is staring them in the face," Rob McCoy of GTE observes. Other contributors feel that there are times the manager can be of assistance without waiting for performance to suffer.

"When I sense a problem," says Alina Bilodeau of The Clorox Company, "I suggest that they use me as a sounding board or phone the Employee Guidance Hotline for help. The manager has to be in tune with the personal happiness of the reps."

Don House of NCR, in contrast, feels that a caring manager can sometimes head off problems before they cause performance drops. "Be genuinely interested in your employees' problems," he advises. "Don't wait for some disaster. This may merely take the form of offering some needed advice, such as when to see a lawyer or how to go about getting some other type of assistance.

"For example, the home of one of my employees was broken into and some personal possessions were stolen. I went to her house (with someone else) and offered my condolences and support. Next I offered advice about police and insurance. I feel a trust relationship was enhanced.

"If problems are more severe, like drinking or marital relationships, most major companies offer programs that are more competent than the manager. The manager need only show concern and support.

"Sales reps look at their managers as advisors and that role shouldn't stop with just business matters. For those individuals who are best motivated by their relationship with their managers, it is essential that they feel the manager's interest in their personal lives. For others who are not motivated in that way, there are varying degrees to which you should get involved. The minimum involvement consists in knowing the names of their spouses and children, the college they attended, and a few of their personal interests. Some of the 'rules of engagement' are:

"Become as involved as the rep wants you to be. They may directly request advice or assistance or subtly hint at their desire for it. If it's a hint and you're unsure of the intent, wait—they'll hint again. If they don't, your assistance is probably no longer required.

"Don't get involved if you're not asked to, or if you sense the rep doesn't want you to. If you try too hard to offer unwanted assistance, it will backfire.

"Always become involved if job performance is affected.

"If you feel there is a serious drug, alcohol, or marital problem, get involved only at the request of the rep or the spouse. Those problems will always affect job performance sooner or later. If you're asked, don't become a therapist—be a friend and help them find the proper professional help, then get out. Otherwise you're likely to get caught in the middle and become part of the problem."

Whether the manager's involvement in a rep's problem is triggered by a drop in performance or by a request from the rep, he or she shouldn't try to be a therapist. Instead, refer the rep to the company's employee assistance organization; if that is not available, the manager can suggest outside sources of help. For example:

- Alcohol or drug abuse: phone 1-800-821-4357 for referrals, twenty-four-hour service.
- Child abuse: National Child Abuse Hotline, 1-800-422-4453, twenty-four hours; also, National Council on Child Abuse and Family Values, 1-800-222-2000, 7:30–4:30 PST.
- Drinking problems: the local chapter of Alcoholics Anonymous may be listed in the local phone book; if not, phone 1-800-944-4768 for information about local assistance.

* Financial problems: in most cities there are free credit counselling services.
* Food abuse: National Food Addiction Hotline, 1-800-872-0088, 8 A.M.–9 P.M. Monday to Friday, 8 A.M.–6 P.M. Saturday and Sunday.
* Marital problems: ask the psych department of the nearest university to suggest sources of assistance.
* Mental health problems: phone the National Mental Health Association, 1-800-969-NMHA for information about local assistance, twenty-four hours.
* Runaway children: National Runaway Switchboard, twenty-four hours, 1-800-621-4000.
* Trauma: American Trauma Society, 1-800-556-7890, Monday through Friday, 9–5 EST.

13

Performance Review and Target Setting

Most human beings have a desire to know the answers to two questions: "How am I doing?" and "What does the future hold for me?"

It's up to sales managers to provide the answers to these questions for their sales reps. But when sellers are asked how their companies inform them of their progress, for far too many the answer is, "I figure no news is good news" or "If I do something wrong, I hear about it soon enough."

Most managers realize the importance of sitting down with each sales rep at regular intervals to review the rep's past accomplishments, set future goals, and discuss ways of reaching them. This process may be called Evaluation and Counselling or Performance Review, among other titles.

A current theory is that if the manager provides adequate feedback during each contact with the sales rep, a more formal, scheduled feedback session is unnecessary. Those who favor the periodic reviews reply that (1) many managers fail to tell reps "how they're doing," despite what the manager's job description says, (2) evaluation discussions during work-with sessions are often brief, held in settings that don't provide adequate privacy, and concentrate on day-to-day matters rather than the long-range career development of the salesperson ("the trees and not the forest").

Despite its obvious importance, the formal evaluation session is an activity that both manager and seller often approach with reluctance and embarrassment. That need not be so.

This chapter summarizes basic principles of the performance review as gleaned by the author in some twenty-five years of training first-line managers and describes specific procedures of a few individual companies.

The Six-Question Review

Six basic questions should be answered, individually, for each seller as completely as possible by the manager.

1. What's my job; that is, what exactly am I supposed to do?

The standard answer to this question is, "Read your job description." But that's usually a rather incomplete answer. Many job descriptions are obsolete, and few of them give a truly accurate picture of all the factors of the job. Moreover, no two sales reps have jobs that are exactly identical. The job varies with the individual, the territory, and the market conditions.

In a study of blue-collar workers, employees were asked to list the four most important functions they were expected to perform. Then their bosses were asked to list the four most important tasks their subordinates performed. The correlation between the two lists was only 35 percent!

So the wise manager is continually making sure that the job, as the manager sees it, is the same as the job the sales rep sees. The performance review helps to do this.

"Studies show that the highest motivator is the understanding of 'how I contribute' to the success of the organization," Rob McCoy of GTE points out. "This knowledge is an essential part of 'what's my job.'"

2. *How* am I supposed to do it?

The answer to this question comes, of course, with training—not just headquarters training and national sales meetings, but the manager's continuing on-the-job training.

3. How *well* am I supposed to do it?

Many companies fail to answer this question fully. They set quotas on sales volume and on calls per week but don't define what's expected on other aspects of the sales position.

The rep may be meeting quotas on both calls and sales, but what about opening new accounts? Handling customer complaints or special requests? Reporting on field conditions and competitive activity? Using the entertainment allowance effectively? Submitting reports that are accurate and on time?

Asking somebody to do something without providing some measure of success is like telling a high jumper to practice without providing the horizontal bar, or asking a golfer not to keep score.

Many salespeople resent the fact that the only standard imposed upon them is the number of calls per day or per week. "Quality of calls is more important than the sheer number of calls," they insist. "I'd rather make two good calls a day than six lousy ones." And they tell the story about the rep who made twenty-eight calls in one day and would have hit thirty except that a couple of prospects asked him what he was selling.

Performance standards can be developed for many more aspects of the selling job in addition to just calls made. Depending upon the nature of the selling, standards can be set for such things as:

- Percentage of calls on customers that result in orders.
- Average dollar sale per call.
- Average number of products sold per call.
- Percentage of prospect calls resulting in an initial order.
- Percentage of calls resulting in a demonstration.
- Percentage of demonstrations resulting in an order.
- Percentage of calls resulting in a request for proposal.
- Percentage of proposals resulting in orders.
- "The most critical of all," one manager adds, "is customer satisfaction and loyalty generated by the sales force. This can be measured in several ways: percentage of repeat orders, infrequency of complaints, and customer satisfaction as revealed by surveys."

For each task listed on the job description, the manager should be able to complete this sentence: "You're handling this part of your job satisfactorily when . . ." and then follows some objective, observable, or measurable condition that defines adequate performance.

It's important to distinguish between performance standards, on the one hand, and goals, targets, or objectives, on the other. Performance standards define the minimum expected performance on some aspect of the job. Anything below this level is unsatisfactory.

Goals or targets apply to "open-ended" aspects of the job, such as total sales achieved, which vary from sales rep to sales rep and on which there is almost no ceiling.

"I use standards to evaluate everyone on the basic job responsibilities," says one manager, "but after that I evaluate reps on what they have done 'above and beyond' the basic standards.

"Individually set goals, tailored to the rep and the territory, instills accountability and pride in the sales rep."

4. and 5. How am I doing? and What should I do to improve my results?

These two points are covered in the performance review and counselling session, discussed later in the chapter.

6. What's in it for me if I do?

What reward will the sales rep get for improving results? More money, certainly, if there's an incentive element in the compensation plan. But, as noted in Chapter 5, the savvy sales manager knows which additional goodies motivate each individual rep and arranges to reward superior performance with recognition, challenges, opportunities, contest prizes, or whatever it is that motivates each individual.

Reviewing Performance

Scheduled, formal sessions to review performance and set goals are usually held quarterly. Under some circumstances they may be held semiannually or even annually. However, advises Jack Woods of United States Cellular, negative performance should be handled at the time it occurs and not saved for the performance review. Alina Bilodeau of Clorox agrees that although the scheduled sessions are important, the manager must be sufficiently flexible to make interim changes as frequently as necessary.

The review of past accomplishments—successes and failures, goals achieved and goals missed—cannot be effective unless based upon previously agreed-upon standards and targets. If the rep feels proud of the fact that he sold X dollars of Product Y, and the manager tells him he should have sold 2X, the obvious result is frustration and demotivation.

In dealing with a new hire, or in holding this type of review session for the first time, the manager should clarify any existing minimum standards and then jointly agree upon targets or goals for the open-ended aspects of the job. It's a good idea to ask the sales rep what targets seem reasonable—but reps will often come up with goals that are unreasonably high.

Two important points about these goals should be stressed:

1. They must be attainable, but only with effort. Goals set so high as to be unreachable don't motivate sales reps—they frustrate them. Creampuff goals, in contrast, don't induce that extra effort the manager is trying to encourage.

"Too often salespeople offhandedly establish unrealistically high goals," notes Dave Singer of Cellular One. "Have them filter their goals through a thought process involving the number of calls they can make, the backlog they have in place, and the closing rate they can achieve. They will come up with a much more realistic target, one that they can buy into."

2. Goals should deal with that rep's activities, not his or her personality. Beware of subjective goals such as "initiative," "company loyalty," "co-operation" and other qualities reminiscent of the Boy Scout oath. If the sales rep feels he has been especially cooperative and the manager grades him low on that target, the review process can do more harm than good. Remember: performance, not personality.

The Interview

Assuming that the rep and the manager have agreed upon clearly defined performance goals in the past, here are some pointers on conducting the interview:

1. Both manager and sales rep prepare for the interview in advance by reviewing notes on the previous session and collecting information on accomplishments since then. Some companies provide forms that the manager and sales rep fill out in advance.

2. The manager provides a place for the interview that assures privacy and no interruptions. This session is too important to be conducted over a dinner table or in the front seat of a car.

3. After some chitchat to create a relaxed atmosphere, the manager will often open the interview by complimenting the seller on successes.

4. Turning to areas in which performance has not been up to expectations, the manager asks probing questions that force the seller to analyze reasons for the disappointing results. The manager readily acknowledges the existence of any obstacles over which the seller has no control, but uses questions to get the seller to recognize any shortcomings in his or her own performance.

5. Manager and seller jointly agree upon action steps to remedy the deficiency. This will often include steps to be taken by the manager, such as enrolling the rep in a training program or providing some specialized field coaching. It will also include the rep's recognition of the need for changing some aspects of his or her sales methods or work patterns.

"The agreement," Robert McCoy of GTE points out, "may also include actions to be taken by the manager to improve sales success, such as improving service, shortening the delivery cycle, or getting advertising or promotional support."

6. The manager and the rep mutually work out targets for the forthcoming period.

7. At the end of the session, the manager gets feedback by asking the rep to summarize their decisions. This step is too often omitted. The manager assumes that the rep's perception of the interview is the same as the manager's—which is rarely the case. After asking for feedback, the manager may be shocked at the lack of correspondence between the two viewpoints. But it's much better to discover this discrepancy and correct it than to falsely assume that the rep has "gotten the message."

8. At the end of the interview, or a day or so later, there should be a written summary of the decisions reached. Many companies provide a form that is filled in and signed by both parties at the end of the interview. If this is not the case, the manager can mail a summary to the rep a day or so later.

Procedures of Specific Companies

Following are participants' discussions of their company procedures.

Bill Hammick, McKesson Drug Co.:

We have a written review once a year with quarterly follow-ups. I first send sales reps the written RIG (responsibility, indicator, goal) form and have them evaluate their own performance as to strengths, areas needing improvement, and plans for the future. Then I write up my own comments and we go over them together.

Bob Higham, CIBA:

The goal-setting process is based on the four basic job functions, which are:

1. *Achieving sales results.*

2. *Demonstrating sales skills and communication skills.* The representative must demonstrate effective selling and communication skills as measured by the district manager's observation of these critical actions: asking for the business and establishing successful trials; preplanning all calls based on specific call objectives; holding a pertinent post-call analysis; and showing effective and relevant use of product and compet-

itive product knowledge. Preplanning would be evaluated by how aware the representative is of competitive movements or shifts in business and whether he or she is taking action in response. That would include ensuring adequate inventory, prestocking new products, handling returns, and recording all pertinent data so they are readily available for future calls.

3. *Implementing promotional programs and using any sales aids effectively.*

4. *Demonstrating effective territory management.*

Based on these job functions, there are six steps in the goal-setting process:

1. When goals are set, they should reflect the overall aims of the company, which include increasing productivity as well as sales.

2. Goals should be defined in such a way as to pay off obviously with significant results.

3. Goals set in key areas should be specific and prioritized.

4. Goals should be written with a concrete goal statement and include a specific objective and action plan for each goal.

5. An action plan should be developed.

6. A review system should be established.

There are actually four different kinds of goals: 1) the routine or ordinary goals essential to acceptable job performance; 2) problem-solving goals, to restore a situation to normal; 3) innovative goals in new areas, which call for creativity and ingenuity; and 4) personal development goals, established to ensure career growth.

Basically, goals should be set once or twice a year. There can be short-term goals for one or two months and long-term goals, usually for one year, which can be reviewed periodically and adjusted after six months if necessary.

Goal-setting is a two-way street. The representative and the manager must get together and agree on a specific goal. Once the goal is set, there are other steps to follow in committing it to paper. First is the attainment, or action, step, by the district manager: what the manager must do to ensure that the representative achieves his or her goals; second is the attainment step by the representative; third is the measurement criteria to be put down by the manager; fourth is the measurement criteria for the representative; and fifth is the review dates, agreement on how often these goals will be reviewed by the manager and representative. In my case, a review occurs on each field contact with the rep, usually every two months.

Jerry McCloskey, Heinz U.S.A.:

Take note of the Heinz performance appraisal (Figure 13-1) that is executed by the manager and representative annually but can be revised whenever the situation warrants.

Too often, there is agreement on improvement objectives but never an update as to how the goals are to be achieved. This form dictates to each level of supervision just how, when, and where each goal is to be fulfilled.

At Heinz the emphasis is on retail store coverage, out-of-stocks, new items sold, facings gained, and displays sold. This is one aspect of the job that is monitored by a monthly reporting system and it gives immediate feedback on job performance.

The balance between qualitative and quantitative goals is a fine line. No good manager wants quantity without quality. The cost of fielding a rep dictates emphasis on preparation, objectives, and results, but one should not lose sight of the customer and the long-term benefits of a complete call.

Follow-up appraisals should start on the positive and reinforce accomplishments, then delve in the hard-to-accomplish areas.

The "what's-in-it-for-me" answers should be clear to entry-level recruits. As they progress, they gain a clear understanding of future goals and upward progress on the success ladder. Egos must come into play and be stroked. No good salesperson is lacking a competitive spirit. It must be fed and nurtured for the short term (monetary) and focused on the long term (advancement).

Performance, not personality, is a gray area. Managers must deal with the unorthodox but not expect perfectly imaged people in the boss's likeness. Territories require specific types of personalities and dictate different managerial focus as well.

Compensation goals in the way of semiannual incentives focus on case targets and category sales performance. Annual goals can contain overriding goals that specify expense reduction, upper management goals, and customer contact (business reviews, new item distribution, and so on). All in all, the balance must be fair both to the company and the employee, regardless of level. Industry norms are available to monitor internal systems to provide competitive benchmarks for the company. It should be an annual project of management to watch the company's rank within its industry.

Figure 13-1.   Sample performance appraisal form.

HEINZ U.S.A.
PERFORMANCE APPRAISAL

A PROGRAM TO <u>PROVIDE</u> <u>FEEDBACK</u> ON

JOB PERFORMANCE

Name (Last, First)				Date
Social Security Number	Chk. Digit	Location	Job Title	
Covering Period From			To	
Supervisor's Signature				Date
Employee's Signature				Date
Reviewed By:				Date

Form E-340   8/87   EMPLOYMENT DEPARTMENT — RETAIN 1 YEAR

(continued)

Figure 13.1. *Continued.*

Major Job Responsibilities (No More Than 10)	*NUMERICAL RATING FACTORS 5 = Far Exceeds Requirements 4 = Exceeds Requirements 3 = Fully Meets Expectations 2 = Needs Immediate Improvement 1 = Unacceptable	Numerical Rating Factor (See Chart*) *Use Only Whole Numbers*	Percent Of Job Importance Total 100%	Performance Rating Col. 1 x Col. 2
1 Achieve District's case sales objectives		x	40%	=
Supporting Statement:				
2 Assure effective HQ and retail coverage		x	10%	=
Supporting Statement:				
3 Maintain a favorable variance to District budget		x	5%	=
Supporting Statement:				
4 Training, development and evaluate personnel		x	15%	=
Supporting Statement:				
5 Development of new business opportunities		x	10%	=
Supporting Statement:				
6 Accomplish monthly SAS coverage		x	5%	=
Supporting Statement:				
7 Enforcement of Company's policy on business conduct		x	5%	=
Supporting Statement:				
8 Develop meaningful customer relationships		x	10%	=
Supporting Statement:				
9		x		=
Supporting Statement:				
10		x		=
Supporting Statement:				

EVALUATION RATINGS

4.5 – 5.0 = Far Exceeds Requirements
3.6 – 4.4 = Exceeds Requirements
2.7 – 3.5 = Fully Meets Expectations
1.8 – 2.6 = Needs Immediate Improvement
1.0 – 1.7 = Unacceptable

100%	Total Rating
	Overall Evaluation

```
|-----------|-----------|-----------|-----------|-----------|
1           2           3           4           5
Unacceptable  Needs Immediate  Fully Meets  Exceeds   Far Exceeds
              Improvement      Expectations  Requirements  Requirements
```

EMPLOYEE ACTION SHEET

Personal Action Plan:

It may be necessary to create several action sheets to address different goals and/or problem areas where improvement or development is needed.) Action Sheets are to be completed by the employee: They are kept by the employee and can be reviewed by the supervisor and employee as needed. This is a "working" Action Sheet and can be amended as necessary.

Brief statement of goals/problems/improvements/development needs -

Obstacles you will encounter -

Training and support you will require - (Note: Please communicate training needs to the Personnel Department.)

Identify those who can assist you -

Set time deadlines -

Form E-340   Insert Reverse Side

(continued)

Figure 13.1.   *Continued.*

GOALS FOR EVALUATION PERIOD

Use the Goal Statement Section below to designate high-impact goals or personal development goals that you need to work toward during the next evaluation period. These goals should flow from the job responsibility discussion on page 2. These goals may be accomplished sooner than the end of the evaluation period. If so, you may wish to work on other goals. LCO projects, TQM projects, the implementation of new technology (e.g., P.C.'s) may all be goals that can be achieved. Goal-setting should promote creativity and define accountability. Before entering the goal below, please apply the test listed below. Goal outcomes can be included in the ratings section on page 2. An Employee Action Sheet may be a good place for you to begin organizing your goal plan.

*Apply the following test to all goals. Are they:

REALISTIC	UNDERSTANDABLE	MEASURABLE	BEHAVIORAL	AGREED UPON

Goal Statement: _____

_____

_____

_____

Anticipated Completion Date

Goal Statement: _____

_____

_____

_____

Anticipated Completion Date

Goal Statement: _____

_____

_____

_____

Anticipated Completion Date

Total Quality Management Involvement Goal: _____

_____

_____

_____

Anticipated Completion Date

Form E-340   Insert 8/88   EMPLOYEE - PREPARE 1 COPY AND RETAIN

PERFORMANCE TRAITS FEEDBACK

Use this sheet to designate development needs as well as strengths. These traits represent core job related behaviors, so please evaluate each. Use the space provided to explain and/or describe how the person handles each trait. Employees may wish to complete an Action Sheet for ones needing improvement.

	Better Performance Traits Than Required For This Job	Performance Traits Are At The Fully Acceptable Level	Performance Traits Need Further Development
Adaptability: Adjusting to new or changing requirements and major unforeseen situations.	☐	☐	☐
e.g. —			
Analytical Ability: Acquiring and evaluating data, problems and/or opportunities necessary to achieve goals.	☐	☐	☐
e.g. —			
Communication Skill: Verbal expression of ideas clearly and convincingly. Writing clearly and concisely.	☐	☐	☐
e.g. —			
Control: Maintaining the constant awareness of projects necessary to direct them to successful completion.	☐	☐	☐
e.g. —			
Subsidiarity: Delegating the responsibility for decision-making and action to those who are "on the firing line."	☐	☐	☐
e.g. —			
Energy Level: Demonstrating the ability and willingness to go the additional mile to accomplish one's goals.	☐	☐	☐
e.g. —			
Initiative: Self-starting and self-directing often demonstrated through seeking new responsibilities, solutions and challenges.	☐	☐	☐
e.g. —			
Judgement: Preparing and making objective, timely, cost-effective business decisions that lead to the achievement of goals.	☐	☐	☐
e.g. —			
Human Relations Skills: Establishing productive working relationships that deal cooperatively and effectively with people at all levels.	☐	☐	☐
e.g. —			
Planning/Organizing: Anticipating needs, determining activities and actions, and setting priorities necessary to achieve goals.	☐	☐	☐
e.g. —			
Job Knowledge: Technical competence, understanding and proficiency in one's profession.	☐	☐	☐
e.g. —			
Other (Specify and Explain):	☐	☐	☐
e.g. —			
Other (Specify and Explain):	☐	☐	☐
e.g. —			

- 3 -

(continued)

Figure 13.1. *Continued.*

COMMENTS SHEET

FEEDBACK AND COMMENTS ON PERFORMANCE, WORK BEHAVIORS AND THE PERFORMANCE APPRAISAL PROCESS

This section should include specific comments and suggestions related to work behavior and job performance. It may also be used for specific comments related to personal development plans and to the performance appraisal process itself.

Supervisor Comments:

Employee Comments:

Howard Strelsin, Terminix International:

Counseling and field coaching overlap. Terminix does not have an annual review procedure; we believe regular daily, weekly, and monthly or bimonthly reviews are better.

I have developed what I call the "plateau theory" of sales rep development. If the manager works with his or her people on an "as needed" basis, this is what you see: during initial training, performance slopes upward. Then, when the manager neglects the field management responsibility, things start to drop. So the manager gets involved again and sales go up to the original plateau level but no higher. Then sales drop, go back up to the original plateau, and you have a stagnant performance because the manager gets involved on an as-needed basis.

The effective manager has a consistent program of helping the rep to develop and carries out the program in a way that motivates rather than demotivates. In Terminix, the program has these three components:

1. *The daily review.* Our daily check-in accountability session each morning allows the manager to spend five to ten minutes with each of the four or five reps looking at yesterday's results and today's game plan. Sales reps come into the office first thing every morning, handing in yesterday's report and their plans for the day. This is the best time for the manager to review problems such as closing or time management. If the manager sees that the rep traveled 120 miles that day, the manager will ask what might have been done differently.

2. *The weekly development review.* Once a week the manager holds a longer personal development review with each rep. They review trends: what's the sales volume compared with the goals the rep has set for him- or herself? What's the percentage of leads closed? How many "creative sales" were there—that is, sales where the rep developed the lead?

If the salesperson is falling behind the goals he or she set, the manager determines whether the problem is skills or work habits. If the latter, for example, the manager might ask the rep during the next week to average one more call a day. The goal is not too far from the present level, "not from A to Z but just from A to B." If the problem is skills, the manager may use role-playing to review sales methods.

Sales Rep A, for example, might be seeing ten people a day, averaging four or five proposals a day, and selling one job. Sales Rep B might see only six or seven people but make six proposals and sell two or three jobs.

When goals aren't met, there's either a behavior or attitude problem, or a skills problem. Either they know what to do and just don't do it, or they don't know how to do it. In these weekly one-on-one sessions, we review the trends and tie them back to the goals the rep set at the beginning of the year. Then we set specific goals for the coming week.

The follow-up is just as important. "Joe, on Tuesday I'd like to spend some time with you. I'll do some demonstrating in the morning and watch you in the afternoon."

3. *The written field sales evaluation.* Terminix branch managers are asked to do a formalized, written field sales evaluation of each rep every thirty to sixty days. The criteria include:

* Image
* Preparedness, or organizational skills
* Presentation skills
* Professionalism
* Prospecting (creative ability)
* Closing techniques

There's a brief curbside conference after each call, but all the above criteria are evaluated at the end of the day.

During the day the manager picks three or four major items of concern and may work on one or two to improve them. You can't change everything all at once, especially with a veteran sales rep who has been accustomed to doing things a certain way.

The most important aspect of this kind of session is for the manager to act more as a moderator to get the rep to gain his or her own insights as to what might have been done differently on each call. You can't just tell someone, "You need to do this, and you need to do that." It's more important that the manager ask the right questions to get the rep to realize what should have been done differently.

This type of counseling and coaching creates an environment in which everybody feels good about the company, the branch manager, and themselves, because they can actually see the improvement they're making. There's a competitive spirit—everybody wants to beat everybody else—but it's a friendly competitive spirit; they also want to help one another.

Andy Anderson, G. D. Searle:

We review performance in two phases: a field contact report and a formal annual view.

The field contact report: Every time a district sales manager works with a representative, he submits a formal, two-page report. This is just between the representative and the district sales manager. The regional director may review these reports from time to time in the district manager's file.

The field contact report is a sort of mini performance evaluation, a record of what the manager observed and what forward action has been prescribed. The manager will review the previous report on the next visit and during the annual review will recap all of them. In this way there are no surprises at the annual review; counseling is an ongoing rather than a once-a-year process.

The annual performance evaluation: This is a formalized report four pages long, and it does go into the rep's personnel folder.

How can the sales manager assure acceptance of the annual recommendations? First, the manager has to understand the difference between behavior and personality. It's pretty tough for me to start criticizing you as a person, but it should be fairly easy for me to give you constructive suggestions on some of your behavior.

We stress that managers look at behavior, not personality. We spend a lot of time on this, and our managers don't make comments like "You're lazy." It's one thing to say you're not making enough calls, but it's another thing to say you're lazy.

If the goals are set right—and we live and die by the budget—if you're below budget you know something's wrong. To arrive at the budget figures, we have an index of potential on each product group. Everybody's involved in setting the budget figures—the district managers, the regional directors—and the reps clearly understand how the numbers were determined. The rep may not agree with them, but we avoid that old truism, "If you let reps set their own budgets, they'll set it higher than you will."

14

Incentive Plans

"Money," one sales manager notes, "is not the only thing that motivates salespeople, but it's a long way ahead of whatever is in second place."

Money isn't even mentioned as a prime motivator in Maslow's hierarchy of values (Chapter 5), but it is the medium by which the seller wins all of those Maslow values: security, recognition, esteem, self-actualization.

"Remember that money is not the only thing that drives people," cautions Dave Singer of Cellular One. "Employee surveys that rank the importance of motivating factors always place recognition and a sense of accomplishment above income."

"Many people are not driven primarily by dollars," agrees Jack Woods of United States Cellular. "The manager needs to have a good feel for the main motivators of each person on the team. The ideal incentive compensation program should have some flexibility so the manager can adjust it for each team member."

"Incentive plans should have very quantitative and measurable objectives, preferably sales dollars, with a timely payout upon achievement," advises Craig Hattabaugh of Aspen Technology. "The objective of an incentive plan is to motivate people to work harder and smarter and thus generate additional business. If this isn't your objective, save yourself the hassle of administering an incentive plan and just pay higher base salaries."

Even with an effective compensation plan, says Don House of NCR, "some people rise to a certain level of income and then become happy and satisfied. It is important to identify these people. Your company may suffer by having this type of person tie up good territory where someone more ambitious would be more productive.

"Another type of salesperson," he adds, "is one who is so greedy that he or she will pull almost any deal or trick on the customer of the company for personal benefit. These people will ruin your company's reputation and make it difficult or even impossible for someone to follow them."

Money itself may be the key motivator to some individuals, as Tim Duncan of American Greetings points out in this example: "I managed a sales rep a few years ago who was extremely money motivated. He would even go so far as to figure his potential bonus earnings at the end of each day and total them at the end of the week. He kept a graph on the wall behind his desk as a constant reminder of where he stood against financial goals.

"He thought he was motivated by a desire to be promoted into management, but that urge was minuscule compared with his thirst for money. He needed to change his goals. After he sold a customer, he began to concentrate on the next customer and forgot about servicing the old ones. He was constantly behind the eight ball and refused to see why he was there."

Motivating the sales rep to focus on part of the job at the expense of other parts is only one of the pitfalls to be avoided in designing the incentive plan. There are a number of basic principles to be followed, according to most of our contributors.

1. *No compensation plan is a substitute for effective sales management.* It might seem that a seller on a straight commission basis, with income directly related to sales effectiveness, would do everything right. But commission-only salespeople, like those on salary or salary-plus plans, can be guilty of making poorly planned calls, spending too much time on friendly but unprofitable prospects, or wasting valuable selling hours on nonproductive activities.

No matter what the compensation plan, the sales force needs training, coaching, supervision, and all the other aspects of motivation noted in Chapter 5. Although an effective incentive plan is an important element in the motivational mix, it's possible to have poorly motivated sales reps on a commission basis and highly motivated reps on a straight salary. A good incentive plan is an important plus, but not the only ingredient.

2. *Design the plan around the total job.* "The most important aspect of a compensation plan is to design it around the description of the position," Tim Duncan of American Greetings notes. "In that way you pay the highest awards to those who do the total job well.

"Today many companies restructure their sales forces and do not change the incentive plans to fit the changing job. If the position is essentially a sales position, pay the reps for sales effort. If the position is a mixture of sales and service, mix their bonus proportionately, that is, if the job is 60 percent sales and 40 percent service, design the compensation plan to reflect that.

"If your company is totally dependent upon the sales reps for revenue, then pay them for bringing in sales, perhaps a straight commission with a draw. If your company relies on reorders based on your reputation for quality and service, pay them a salary for the service work and a commission for the sales work. In short, pay them for the job you want them to do.

"And in selecting new sales reps, it's not only essential to get the right person for the job, but also the person who will fit the compensation plan you're offering and work well within it. The rep who thrives on a straight commission is a totally different person from the one who prefers a salary."

"An effective sales organization results from an agreement upon goals and upon the strategies for reaching them," adds Jerry McCloskey of Heinz U.S.A. "Compensation plans motivate people to reach those goals, but they should not be substituted as a goal. Keep the reps reminded of the goals by means of tracking reports, incentive standings, and brag sheets. These motivate the sales force to strive to attain management's goals."

3. *The trend is toward salary plus incentive.* Over the past half-century, there has been a steady trend away from straight-commission plans to compensation plans with a straight salary plus some incentive for productivity. The incentive payment may be a commission (calculated as some percentage of sales volume) or a bonus (calculated by some other formula).

Commission-only plans tend to be found in types of selling where little training is required and there is a high turnover among the sales force.

Salary-only plans are found where the selling process involves so many people that it is impossible to assign individual credit, or where the plan would be so complicated that administration would be costly.

4. *Reward for profits, not volume.* Any plan based on sales volume rather than profit contribution is likely to motivate the sales force to concentrate on those products and services that are easiest to sell, even though more total profit would be generated by devoting more effort to more profitable products that are harder to sell.

As an example, let's say that a new product line, A, contributes 40 percent of each sales dollar to overhead and profit, whereas an older commodity-type product, B, contributes only 20 percent. Assume that a sales rep has a quota of $750,000 in sales volume per year, with a commission of 1 percent on sales over quota.

His present sales volume (Table 14-1) is $250,000 in Product A and $500,000 in Product B.

Motivated by the incentive program, the rep determines to invest additional time and effort. Since it takes about 50 percent more time to sell the A line than the B line, the rep can sell either $300,000 additional B products or $200,000 additional A products.

If the B product is pushed (Table 14-2), the rep will sell an additional $300,000 of it for a total of $800,000, generate a $260,000 contribution, and earn a bonus of $3,000 (1 percent of the $300,000 over the $750,000 quota).

If the more profitable A product is pushed (Table 14-3), the rep will sell an additional $200,000 of it for a total of $450,000, generate $280,000 in contribution, but receive only a $2,000 bonus. As a reward for increasing the company's profit by $20,000, the rep is penalized $1,000.

Emphasis on the more profitable products doesn't mean that the

Table 14-1. Present sales.

Product	Sales Volume	% Contri- bution	$ Contri- bution	Bonus
A	$250,000	40%	$100,000	—
B	500,000	20%	100,000	—
TOTAL	$750,000	—	$200,000	—

Table 14-2. Emphasis on Product B.

Product	Sales Volume	% Contri- bution	$ Contri- bution	Bonus
A	$ 250,000	40%	$100,000	—
B	800,000	20%	160,000	—
TOTAL	$1,050,000	—	$260,000	$3,000

Table 14-3. Emphasis on Product A.

Product	Sales Volume	% Contri- bution	$ Contri- bution	Bonus
A	$450,000	40%	$180,000	—
B	500,000	20%	100,000	—
TOTAL	$950,000	—	$280,000	$2,000

less profitable ones can be neglected. The goal is the most profitable balance between more time on the A's and less time on the B's.

To motivate the sales force to strive for this balance, reports Andy Anderson of G. D. Searle, "specific product weightings are determined for each quarterly incentive period. For example, in one quarter Product A was weighted at 65 percent and Product B at 35 percent. In this manner we were able to allocate the incentive dollars and reward for profit contribution according to the goals and direction of senior management. Field sales personnel were able to see where the emphasis in effort would produce the most profit dollars."

The compensation plan can motivate sales reps to adjust their allocation of effort for the different seasons of the year. For example, Jerry McCloskey reports that Heinz U.S.A. designates three key periods with differing goals for each. They are:

1. The first fiscal quarter is the "fast start" period, with emphasis on attaining the necessary volume and market share.
2. During the second quarter there are seasonal summer objectives, plus semiannual volume targets.
3. During the second half of the fiscal year, special goals and objectives are established to ensure that the year's targets are met.

"In other words," McCloskey explains, "we target three key periods and reward the sales reps accordingly. The sales volume goals represent 75 percent of the incentive plan payout, the balance being focused on total job responsibilities: business reviews, account planning sessions, control of sales expenses, and customer deductions. In addition, for field reps and midmanagers, there is a "retail condition recognition" system with rewards for in-store accomplishments like effective departments, displays, and distribution."

Plans that stress profit contribution should not be confused with plans sometimes used in smaller companies, in which sales reps receive some share of company profits. Compensation derived from profit is an excellent program if the persons receiving the bonus can truly control the costs. If the costs are beyond their control, the plan is not fair.

5. *Individual or pooled?* Where it is possible to measure individual results, most companies have found it more effective to reward each seller on the basis or his or her sales than to offer everyone a share in a pool. G. D. Searle, for example, whose sales reps call on doctors, can still measure individual results based on a service that checks drugstore prescriptions and hence rewards performance on an individual basis.

Pooled plans can be effective where sellers work closely together, as in a retail store, and the outstanding performers are motivated to help coach the less effective ones in order to build up the size of the pool. Dave Singer, for one, feels that "the more you can have a team compensation plan, the better for all concerned."

6. *How big a bonus?* "As big as possible within the financial re-straints of the company," remarks Tim Duncan of American Greetings. "Nothing is more disheartening than to lose a good employee to a competitor that offers a better bonus plan.

"A sales rep will be better motivated by a plan that has no ceiling. If there is a ceiling, the rep will be inclined to stop selling when the ceiling is reached, holding potential sales in reserve for the next incentive period."

Being stingy in designing an incentive plan can be a costly mistake. If the bonus is not big enough to stimulate the sales force to exert extra efforts, it is simply money given away for nothing.

A reasonable rule of thumb is to say that the top earner should be able to earn an incentive payment of about 90 percent of the base salary. In G. D. Searle, for example, 20 percent of the sales force earn at least one-third of their base salary in bonus.

7. *How frequently?* "As often as possible," says Tim Duncan.

An annual bonus is always welcome, but the thought of a bonus in December is not a big motivator during the preceding January or February. Incentives work best if the sales force can look forward to getting its rewards every month or every quarter.

If the incentive payment is far in the future, it can be made more motivational with the use of interim reports showing each rep how much he or she has earned so far.

8. *The total sales job.* Incentive payments are rarely based on total sales volume. The plan can be devised to encourage the sales force to do a balanced, year-round selling job.

For example, if it's important for the sellers to sell all product lines "across-the-board," the incentive can be reduced or eliminated if the rep does not sell, for example, 80 percent of quota on all product lines. Searle's "product weighting" program encourages the representatives to work toward achieving budget on all promoted products.

To avoid the temptation to hold up orders and then "load" them into one quarter, the incentive can be higher for reps who attain some reasonable percentage of their annual sales each quarter.

The plan must encourage the optimum balance not only among products but also among various aspects of the job. A booby trap in some plans is that they encourage the sales force to emphasize one aspect of the job while incurring costly neglect of other phases.

"I once managed for a company that paid its sales reps a bonus for minimizing service costs," reports Tim Duncan. "Sales reps were allowed 6 percent of each customer's sales volume in service costs. If they stayed under that percentage, their bonus was increased accordingly. As you might expect, this program backfired by encouraging the reps to hold back on service and let the accounts suffer."

It can also include special bonuses for opening new accounts, introducing new products, and the like.

9. *Keeping the plan up-to-date.* "Never change a compensation plan or bonus plan after the fact," cautions Don House of NCR.

Frequent tinkering with the basic structure of the compensation plan can be highly demoralizing to the sales force, but details of the plan may need frequent fine-tuning.

G. D. Searle reviews its compensation plan annually, soliciting ideas from regional sales directors and district sales managers. Last year, for example, they found it desirable to lower the threshold levels at which these managers started to receive volume incentives. The same amount of incentive dollars was available, but it was available at more attainable performance levels.

It's also important to get your sales reps' reactions to your existing plan, or suggestions for revisions in it.

Most sales managers will agree with the comment of Dave Singer of Cellular One: "Keep the plan as simple as possible. If a rep can't understand it in five minutes of study, it's ineffective."

"Keep it simple and direct," advises Tom Dunning of Datacard Corp. "If it is so complicated that it requires a Philadelphia lawyer to figure it out, it will appear arbitary and will not push your sales force in the direction you want them to go.

"Salespeople will figure out what pays the best and will concentrate on that. If the manager is in favor of motherhood and free lunch for orphans, pay for it and don't just talk about it. The best way for managers to evaluate a compensation plan is to ask themselves how they would behave if they were selling under it."

15

Sales Contests

 "Sales contests are not only an excellent form of additional compensation, but they are also a tremendous motivator for the entire force," says Tim Duncan of American Greetings. "A contest is a great vehicle for motivating people who are money-motivated or prize-motivated, for those who are striving for recognition, and for those motivated by fear of failure (they feel that they must win). Good salespeople thrive on contests."

"Local sales contests initiated within the district or region tend to build a competitive spirit if handled correctly," agrees Jerry McCloskey of Heinz U.S.A. "Equitable or fair quotas or benchmarks must be creditable or the whole reason for the contest is lost. Local contests can motivate the reps to keep a sharper eye on the local needs of the first-line manager."

"Contests can be an effective way to focus attention for a short time period," comments Craig Hattabaugh of Aspen Technology. "The scale of the prize should be consistent with the incentive plan. If the prize is too small, people will ignore it. Too large, and you may draw resources aways from everyday tasks. Also, contests should be the exception, not the rule. If you are constantly having contests, something is wrong with your incentive plan."

This chapter deals primarily with local contests designed by the first-line manager to supplement the company's nationwide contests. Most of the comments apply as well to contests run by a smaller company for its entire sales force.

Determining the Objective

The first and very important decisions the first-line manager must make are: What is the purpose of this contest? What am I trying to achieve?

"To increase sales" is not specific enough. If the contest payoff is based on total sales volume, will it shift effort to high-volume, low-profit products at the expense of more profitable ones? Or if the goal is to increase sales in a specific product, will the contest interfere with the across-the-board selling job? How will this local contest relate to, or supplement, the companywide contests?

With these considerations in mind, the local manager can supplement the national contests by designing ones that address the problems specific to this district. Typical goals might be:

- To increase sales on a product in which the district is lagging behind the company.
- To open more new accounts of a specific type.
- To stimulate the launching of a new product.

"Sales contests designed by district managers are an excellent motivational tool as long as the focus of the contest mirrors the focus of the company," notes Andy Anderson of Searle. "Last year our product weightings changed quarterly, based upon the company goals and the corporate mission. For local contests to be effective from a corporate perspective, they should consider the changes in product emphasis from quarter to quarter.

"Additionally, we would recommend that contests managed at the local level be for a nominal amount (that is, less than $500). Contests deemed to have a value greater than $500 would be managed more effectively at headquarters."

"I believe in contests even if the prizes are small," adds Tim Duncan. "To the salesperson, the recognition is just as important as, if not more important than, the prize itself. Local sales contests, which I tried to run at least twice a year, are not difficult to do, even on a small budget."

Howard Strelsin of Terminix International gives an example of how to avoid letting a contest that concentrates on one aspect of selling siphon off too much attention from other aspects of the sales job.

"In the spring we get lots of leads," he says, "so lead closing to us is very important. However, we don't want salespeople to lose their edge on creative business that they bird-dog for themselves. So we put together a contest that says, 'In order to qualify, you must have a 60 percent closing rate, but each rep who qualifies will get an extra bonus for each creative sale made during the contest.'

"We like team contests to develop team spirit. We may pit one part of a city against another, or one city against another, or half of a state against the other half. We make the teams equal by matching the previous sales volume of the team members."

A Question of Fairness

A contest must be fair if it is to motivate all the sales reps. There are two aspects to fairness:

1. *Everybody must have a chance to win.* Contests in which the award goes to the one, two, or three reps who do the "best" or the "most" are ineffective. They motivate the outstanding achievers, who don't need the motivation anyway, and simply frustrate the bottom two-thirds of the sales force, who know they have no chance of winning. The contest must be designed in such a way that everybody has a chance of winning something. This might mean a small merchandise prize or cash award for those who do fairly well and a more valuable merchandise prize or larger cash award for those who do very well.

For example, Dave Singer of Cellular One has quarterly contests in which all members of the 110 Percent Club (those who achieve 10 percent over quota) attend a special meeting for the winners, such as a $50–$100 luncheon, a day of water skiing at a local resort, or a trip to the wine country of California. "It's amazing what this does to the ego of the reps who missed the target and the positive effect it has on their performance in the next quarter. For short contests, I sometimes hand out a $50 or $100 bill to the winner at a sales meeting—not a check, but the actual money."

2. *Everyone must have a nearly equal chance of winning.* This is more difficult to achieve.

If the payoff is based on dollar increases in sales volume, those who already have the highest sales volume will win easily. If it is based on percentage increase, it is loaded in favor of those with the lowest sales volume.

For example, suppose that A, the top sales rep, is selling $100,000 (per day, week, quarter, or whatever) and that Rep B, the lowest or newest, is selling only $25,000. If the award is based on the dollar increase, it will be much easier for A to go from $100,000 or $110,000 than it will for B to go from $25,000 to $35,000.

But if the contest is based on percentage increase, it would be much easier for B to get a 20 percent increase, for $25,000 to $30,000, than it would for A to go from $100,000 to $120,000.

When challenged by their manager to come up with a solution that would be fair to both, one group of sales reps proposed the ingenuous idea of assigning to each rep a "contest unit" equal to the square root of that rep's present sales. The size of the award is based upon the number of contest units accumulated.

In the example above, A would have a contest unit of $316 and B would have a unit of $158. Presumably, it is as easy for A to sell $316 more as it is for B to sell $158 more.

Less mathematical methods of achieving fairness, Tim Duncan suggests, are to base awards on sales increases to established customers, or sales of a particular product to established customers.

"Your people need to feel good about themselves, so make the contest winnable," advises Tom Dunning of Datacard Corp. "Though this may sound like a contradiction, those who have not won should still feel good about their effort and accomplishments despite not winning. 'I'll get 'em next year!' The contest should be fun and interesting but should be a real victory. If everyone wins, it's not a contest."

Follow-up Reminders

For added interest the contest can be built around a theme, such as those suggested as sales meeting themes in Chapter 8.

To get the maximum motivational impact out of the contest, the manager will send out frequent bulletins reminding the force of the awards that can be run and giving the current status of the leaders, of all the reps, or simply of the individual to whom the bulletin is sent.

Quoting Tim Duncan again: "Regardless of their goal, sales contests are tremendous for morale. Just winning and receiving recognition from one's peers may suffice. Prizes do add sweetness to the victory. Many managers set aside budgets for contests, and that is usually the best way. This way prizes can be bigger, such as a color TV, compact disk players, cruises, sports equipment, and so on. If you don't have that type of budget, there is still a lot the local manager can do to establish prizes. Dinner with the manager and the manager's spouse, either in the manager's home or at a nice restaurant, works well. Perhaps the prize can be a modest amount of cash or additional vacation time. Everyone realizes the additional effort put forth during a contest anyway, and extra vacation is a great payoff."

Biographies of Contributors

V. N. (Andy) Anderson, president, North American Operations, G. D. Searle. Joined Searle as VP of sales, 1985, served as executive VP, North American Operations, director of Caribbean Operations, VP U.S. Sales. Former positions include sales rep with S. E. Massengill Co. (1959); E. R. Squibb (1961) as sales representative, sales trainer, director, manager of sales training, director sales administration, regional sales director, and VP sales; group VP marketing at Bristol-Myers Dental Companies; and operated his own consulting firm, Anderson and Associates, specializing in public speaking and marketing training programs. Native of Lindsborg, Kansas; lives with wife, Karen, in Lake Forest, Illinois.

Alina Bilodeau, northeast area sales manager, special markets division, The Clorox Company. BA, Boston College, majors in Economics and Spanish, 1985. With Kraft General Foods, started as sales representative in New York, became sales specialist and key account executive in the New York District, then district manager and district retail manager in the Boston district, and region franchise manager, sales planning, in White Plains, New York. Joined the Clorox Company in 1991.

Tim Duncan, regional sales manager, American Greetings. Former positions include Pickwick International, Inc., Musicland retail division, and selling portable trade show exhibits at Downing Displays. With American Greetings, has been promoted six times. Lives in Atlanta, Georgia, with wife, Cheryl, and three children. Outstanding career accomplishment: has never failed to attain a sales forecast.

Tom Dunning, VP marketing, U.S. sales and marketing, Datacard Corp. BS/BA, Wright State University, Dayton, Ohio. Store manager, Dunhills, Inc.; with Burroughs as sales rep, zone sales manager, district sales manager terminal products, senior marketing coordinator terminal products, branch sales manager, director of research; with Unisys Corp as program manager network application program. Served in U.S. Air Force, 1968–1972.

Stanley M. Evans, owner/operator, Amway distributorship, Wray, Colorado. BA, McCook (NE) Community College. Listed in *Who's Who in Business*, served five years in Army National Guard. Born in Haigler, Nebraska. Wife, Ruth, four children, seven grandchildren.

Kevin A. Flagel, district sales manager, Monsanto Agricultural Company. BS, University of Wisconsin 1972. Born Beaver Dam, Wisconsin.

Bill Hammick, VP, general manager since 1992, McKesson Drug Co., Oklahoma City. AB, University of Nebraska, 1975. Started with McKesson (1975) as sales trainee in Lincoln; service systems representative, Omaha, 1978; sales manager, in St. Louis, for tristate area, 1980; sales manager, Chicago, 1985. Born in Chadron, Nebraska.

Craig Hattabaugh, regional sales manager, Aspen Technology, process modeling technology for process industries. Electrical engineering degree, Worcester Polytechnic Institute, 1981; MBA, Boston University. Nine years with Texas Instruments. Born in Indiana. Lives near Cambridge, Massachusetts, with his wife, Rose, and daughter, Michela.

Robert O. Higham, district manager, CIBA. Attended Youngstown University. 35 years with CIBA. Served in U.S. Navy. Born Youngstown, Ohio.

D. M. (Don) House, district sales manager, NCR, food store industry specialty. Various positions with NCR in southeast U.S. Holds company record for 28 consecutive years of achieving sales quota. Born Charlotte, North Carolina.

Alex D. Jones, market sales manager (19 years), Allstate Insurance Co., Fresno, California. Started career as insurance agent, market sales manager in 1973; manages 34 agents. His district was number one nationally in Allstate in 1990; received Allstate's Key Manager recognition for 13 years. Born Waldron, Arkansas.

Robert S. Layman, district manager, NCR Corporation, Nashville, Tennessee. BS in economics, Vanderbilt University, 1978. Has held sales and sales management positions with NCR. Winner of NCR Chairman's Award three years; number one district in the nation, 1986.

Born Oak Ridge, Tennessee. Lives with wife, Barbara, and son in Brentwood, Tennessee.

G. A. (Jerry) McCloskey, central regional manager, grocery sales, Heinz U.S.A. Degree in administrative management, LaRoche College, Pittsburgh. Career includes sales representative in Boston; account executive in Connecticut; area manager in Tennessee; sales planning manager, headquarters in Pittsburgh; district sales manager, Pittsburgh and Cleveland; marketing manager northeast U.S. Born Boston, Massachusetts.

Judie McCoy, national sales director, Mary Kay Cosmetics. Joined Mary Kay as consultant in 1976, became director in 1978, national sales director in 1991. Number one nationally in sales volume for eight years, number two for two years. Holds company records for highest production in one month and highest production in one year. Born in Milwaukee, lives in Waukesha, Wisconsin.

Robert G. McCoy, assistant VP, premise systems and services, GTE Telephone Operations Group. BS from University of Oregon, where he was a National Science Fellow. Began telecommunications career with AT&T in 1970, held positions in sales, marketing, and operations, branch manager, national accounts. 1986, general sales manager, GTE; subsequently director, business sales and operations, assistant VP, product marketing, assistant VP, premise systems and services; responsible for GTE's deregulated products, services, and operations.

Patrick G. Murphy, director quality, U.S. Marketing Group, NCR, Dayton, Ohio. MBA, University of Dayton.

J. J. (Jim) Nichols, VP, corporate accounts, Dow Chemical USA. Holds science degree in commerce and engineering from Drexel University; postgraduate work in finance at St. Louis University. Joined Dow 1965 as sales trainee; assigned St. Louis as sales representative in Styrofoam Products; 1972, Dow's New York office, district sales manager in functional products and systems department; 1978, product group marketing manager for diagnostic products, Indianapolis. Appointed general sales manager for Dow's Tampa sales office, 1980; 1983, transferred to Cleveland, general sales manager; 1986, VP sales for industrial specialties and services; 1987, VP sales, chemicals and performance products, east central zone; 1990, current position.

William G. Nyberg, president, United Homecraft Inc. Entered home improvement business as part-time telemarketer for R.E.K. Industries, 1970; sales representative, 1972; sales manager, 1975; VP sales,

1980. Started his own company in 1985. Salesman of the Year, 1979. Served in U.S. Army, two-and-a-half years in West Germany.

David A. Ruckman, district director, Merrill Lynch. Ohio State University 1966.

Daniel R. Schnaars, president, FlexCon & Systems, Inc., Lafayette, Louisiana. Born in Pittsburgh, Mr. Schnaars received a BS in mathematics from Mount Union College in 1972. Starting as an insurance salesman, he became state director of Texas for United Companies Life Insurance Company, 1971; territory sales rep for Signode Corporation, 1976; national sales manager, Shipping Systems Inc. of West Monroe, La. In 1985 he started his own company, FlexCon & Systems, which makes bulk bags holding 2,000 pounds of dry chemicals. The firm now sells $8.2 million annually and has 135 employees in its main plant and 31 more in a contract plant.

Lori Schweitzer-Teismann, VP marketing, Olsten Temporaries, Cincinnati, Ohio. Started in 1969, OPW Division, Dover Corp.; Northlic, Stolley Advertising Agency, 1976; account representative, Olsten, 1979; subsequently sales coordinator, assistant VP, sales and marketing. She has held national and local offices of the International Association of Records Management and Administration. A native of Cincinnati, where she lives with her husband, Paul.

David M. Singer, director of sales, Cellular One. BA, business administration, San Francisco State University. Previously district sales manager, National Utility Service, and sales manager/assistant buyer, Macy's San Francisco.

Howard Strelsin, national sales director, Terminix International. BA sociology, Rider College, 1973. Started 19-year career with Terminix as district sales representative in Philadelphia; branch manager, Wilmington, Delaware, and Haverford, Pennsylvania (number one profit margin branch in 1980); regional sales manager of the year three times; division sales manager 1984–1992, now national sales director, coordinating efforts of 1,400 salespeople in 318 service centers.

Charles Williamson, retired sales manager, Nabisco. Born in Fairfield County, Ohio; completed personnel management course at Ohio State University night school. Joined Nabisco as field sales representative in 1953; promoted into sales management with special sales training responsibilities in 1962; sales manager in Dayton, Ohio, 1971; later became sales manager in Columbus, Ohio, in charge of the sales and distribution center. Married Bonnie Stephens, has three daughters. After retirement, moved to St. John, U.S. Virgin Islands, where he operates a children's clothing store and a clothing store for adults.

Jack L. (Woody) Woods, sales manager, United States Cellular, Peoria, Illinois. Attended Victor Valley Community College and Clark County Community College. Previous sales positions with F. D. Titus & Son and R. J. Reynolds. Sales manager for Cellular One in Reno before appointment to present position. Holder of his company's Circle of Excellence Award, both quarterly and annually, and President's Excellence Award, both quarterly and annually, and President's Club. Served five and one half years as sonar technician on Polaris submarine. Born Akron, Ohio.

Index